IN THE KNOW IN

China

LIVING LANGUAGE®

TERRA COGNITA™

Also available from

Business Companion: Chinese

This essential language guide for working with Chinese colleagues is a perfect complement to *In the Know in China*. The 368-page handbook contains more than 1,000 phrases for general business situations and vocabulary for over 25 specific industries, plus a two-way glossary, and handy reference sections. The audio CD contains more than 500 phrases used in realistic business situations.

Handbook/CD program 0-609-60684-0 $21.95/C$32.95
Handbook only 0-609-80629-7 $12.95/C$19.95

Ultimate Mandarin Chinese: Basic-Intermediate

A comprehensive program equivalent to two years of college-level study. Up-to-date conversations and vocabulary in each lesson teach reading, writing, grammar, and culture tips along with conversational skills. Includes a course-book and more than 40 lessons on eight 60-minute cassettes or CDs.

Cassette program 0-517-70877-9 $75.00/C$115.00
Coursebook only 0-609-80065-5 $18.00/C$27.50

300 West 49th Street Suite 314 New York, New York 10019 USA
Phone: 212.663.9890 Fax: 212.663.2404
E-mail: info@terracognita.com
www.terracognita.com

Know Your World

Terra Cognita provides top quality cross-cultural training service and resources. The goal of our cross-cultural learning material is to help you build the awareness and skills to recognize and respect cultural differences you will encounter. Terra Cognita programs thereby ensure a sucessful adjustment to life in a new culture for expatriates and the skills necessary to succeed in international business.

Terra Cognita delivers cross-cultural learning with private seminars and workshops, with online learning modules, and with a variety of video, audio and printed material. Currently Terra Cognita programs meet the needs of expatriates and international business colleagues at various multinational companies, government agencies and educational institutions worldwide.

 LIVE ABROAD! is an innovative video-based expatriate preparation program that covers the entire expatriate experience from preparing to go through the cultural adjustment process to the final return home.

 WORK ABROAD! is a video-based program that explains and vividly re-creates the cross-cultural dynamics of the international business environment.

For more information on Terra Cognita
and a wealth of articles and resources for cross-cultural learning,
visit our Web site at WWW.TERRACOGNITA.COM

V I D E O S   S E M I N A R S   O N L I N E

LIVING LANGUAGE®
A Random House Company

IN THE KNOW IN

CHINA

THE INDISPENSABLE CROSS-CULTURAL GUIDE TO WORKING AND LIVING IN CHINA

WRITTEN BY
Jennifer Phillips

EDITED BY
Christopher Warnasch

Published in the United States by Living Language, A Random House Company

www.livinglanguage.com

Design by Barbara M. Bachman
Illustrations by Adrian Hashimi

Although all factual information in this book, such as Web sites, telephone
numbers, etc., is as up-to-date as possible at press time, changes occur all
the time, and Living Language cannot accept responsibility for the accuracy
of the facts in the book or for inadvertent errors or omissions.

First Paperback Edition

ISBN 1-4000-2045-X

Library of Congress Cataloging-in-Publication Data available

PRINTED IN THE UNITED STATES OF AMERICA

10 9 8 7 6 5 4 3 2 1

ACKNOWLEDGMENTS

Special thanks to Vera Liao, who provided research assistance and answers to a multitude of questions. Thanks as well to the people who generously shared their experiences and input, and to my editor, Chris Warnasch, for his expert guidance. No book is written in a vacuum, and this one would never have happened without the generous support of Richard Davis, with whom I continue a journey toward Terra Cognita. And finally, last on this list, but not in my heart, to Jan, who provided the occasional much-needed kick in the seat and to my family for their support and encouragement.

And thanks to the rest of the Living Language team: Lisa Alpert, Elizabeth Bennett, Helen Tang, Elyse Tomasello, Zviezdana Verzich, Suzanne McGrew, Pat Ehresmann, Denise DeGennaro, Linda Schmidt, Murina Padakis, and Barbara Bachman.

CONTENTS

1. BACKGROUND 21

VITAL STATISTICS 22

CLIMATE 24

PEOPLE 24

CHINESE HISTORY IN BRIEF 26

NOTED (AND NOTORIOUS) CHINESE 34

In Politics 34

In Arts and Literature 36

In Philosophy and Science 37

GOVERNMENT & POLITICS 37

China and Taiwan 39

China's Government 40

The Chinese Communist Party (CCP) 40

The Democratic Parties 40

RELIGION 41

Taoism 42

Confucianism 42

Buddhism 42

Islam 43

HOLIDAYS & FESTIVALS 44

Public Holidays in China 44

Chūn Jié (Spring Festival/Lunar New Year) 45

Yuán Xiāo Jié (Lantern Festival) 46

Qīng Míng Jié (Pure Brightness Day) 46

CONTENTS

Duān Wǔ Jié (Dragon Boat Festival)   47

Zhōng Qiū Jié (Mid-Autumn Festival)   47

Other Festivals and Celebrations   48

EDUCATIONAL SYSTEM   **48**

Preschool Education   49

Primary Education   49

Secondary Education   49

Vocational and Technical Education   50

Post-secondary Education   50

2. CHINA—CULTURE   51

THE CONFUCIAN TRADITIONS OF CHINA   **53**

THE YIN AND YANG OF CHINESE CULTURE **54**

TIME   **55**

Rigid versus Flexible Cultures   56

Chinese-American Interaction   56

Time Tips   57

COMMUNICATION   **58**

Direct versus Indirect Communication   59

Chinese-American Interaction   59

Communication Tips   61

GROUP DYNAMICS   **62**

Group-oriented versus Individualistic   63

Chinese-American Interaction   64

Tips on Group Dynamics   65

STATUS & HIERARCHY   **66**

Ascribed versus Achieved Status   66

Vertical versus Lateral Hierarchy   67

Chinese-American Interaction   68

Tips on Status and Hierarchy   69

RELATIONSHIPS   **70**

Relationship-oriented versus

   Task-oriented   71

Chinese-American Interaction   72

Relationships in China Today   73

RELATIONSHIP TIPS   **74**

REASONING   **74**

Pragmatic, Analytical, or Holistic Reasoning   75

Chinese-American Interaction   77

Feng Shui   77

Tips on Reasoning   78

WHAT DOES IT ALL MEAN?   **79**

3. LIVING ABROAD: THOUGHTS BEFORE YOU GO 81

IMPACT ON CHILDREN   **83**

Infants and Toddlers   85

Preschoolers   86

Preteens   86

Teens   86

IMPACT ON SPOUSES OR PARTNERS   **87**

Giving Up or Postponing a Career   87

Being a Stay-At-Home Parent   88

DUELING CAREERS   **88**

UNDERSTANDING CULTURAL ADAPTATION   **89**

Enchantment   90

Disenchantment   90

Retreat   91

Adjustment   91

And Beyond   92

KEYS TO A SUCCESSFUL ADJUSTMENT   **92**

Coping Techniques   93

FAMILIES   **93**

THE NONWORKING PARTNER   **94**

CHILDREN   **95**

PARENTING ABROAD   **97**

DUAL CAREER COUPLES   98

THE SINGLE LIFE   99

THE GENDER FACTOR   100

THE RACE FACTOR   101

SEXUAL ORIENTATION   102

A WORD ABOUT "EXPATRIATE CLUBS"   102

STAYING IN TOUCH   103

ROUND TRIP TICKET: THE RETURN HOME   104

    Professional Repatriation   *104*

    Personal Repatriation   *105*

    Children's Repatriation   *106*

    Tips for Staying in Touch   *107*

LEARNING ABOUT YOUR NEW HOME   108

MOVING ABROAD "DOS & DON'TS"   110

4. GETTING AROUND IN CHINA   111

ARRIVING IN CHINA   111

BUSINESS TRIPS TO CHINA   113

LEAVING CHINA   114

GETTING AROUND   115

    Driving   *115*

    Taxis   *115*

    Public Transportation   *116*

    Trains   *116*

    Subway   *117*

    Other Options   *117*

TRAVEL TIPS   118

5. LIVING AND STAYING IN CHINA   119

RESIDENCE PERMIT   119

HOUSING   120

    Finding a Living Space   *122*

Moving In   123
Buying Property   124
BRINGING YOUR BELONGINGS   **124**
Appliances and Computers   125
UTILITIES   **126**
TELEPHONES   **127**
Telephone Tips   129
Useful Phone Numbers   129
PETS   **129**
BRINGING YOUR VEHICLE   **131**
Getting a Driver's License   131
SCHOOLS   **132**
SHOPPING   **133**
Where to Shop   134
Service   136
FINANCIAL MATTERS   **136**
Personal Banking   137
SOCIALIZING   **138**
Meeting People and Making Friends   139
Be My Guest. Being on Your
    Best Behavior as a Host or Guest   141
Dating and Beyond   142
Weddings   143
The Three Letters   144
The Six Rituals   144
ETIQUETTE   **146**
General   146
Communicating   147
GIFTS   **149**
ENTERTAINMENT   **151**
HOMOSEXUALITY   **153**
FOOD   **154**
HEALTH AND SAFETY   **155**
Water and Food Tips   158

CONTENTS

CRIME AND LEGAL ISSUES   158
 Emergency Numbers   *159*
POST OFFICE   159
TIPPING   160

6. BUSINESS ENVIRONMENT   161

GOVERNMENT AND BUSINESS   163
THE CHAIN OF COMMAND   164
THE WORK UNIT (*DĀNWÈI*)   165
BUSINESS HOURS   166
OFFICE SPACE   167
WOMEN IN BUSINESS   167
 Tips for Women in Business   *168*

7. BUSINESS STEP-BY-STEP   171

MAKING CONTACT   172
GENERAL BUSINESS ETIQUETTE   174
BUSINESS COMMUNICATION   175
 Telephone   *175*
 E-mail   *176*
GETTING TO THE TOP   177
THE FIRST MEETING   178
MEETING PROTOCOL   178
NEGOTIATING THE DEAL   181
NEGOTIATING TACTICS   184
CLOSING THE DEAL   186
PRESENTING YOUR IDEAS AND
 MAKING SPEECHES   187
BUSINESS ENTERTAINING   189
 Banquet Etiquette   *190*
MANAGING   193

LEAVING A LEGACY   195
A NOTE ON USING INTERPRETERS   196

8. LAST NOTES   199

9. LANGUAGE NOTES   201

APPENDIX A: BEFORE YOU GO   215
APPENDIX B: CONTACTS & RESOURCES   221
APPENDIX C: METRIC CONVERSIONS   227
Index   233

Whether you're moving to China or traveling there for business, it's essential that you know what to expect, and what will be expected of you. Cross-cultural awareness provides you with just that knowledge. Living Language® Terra Cognita™ *In the Know in China* is designed to help both business people and their families navigate the often complex waters of life in another culture. By culture we don't mean Beijing Opera or the writings of Confucius and Lao-tzu. Culture is the backdrop of every activity you engage in and every word you exchange. In China, you'll be dealing with a foreign culture every time you shake a colleague's hand, sit down to write an e-mail, get on a train, or even buy a bowl of rice. A list of "dos & don'ts" provides only part of the picture. A more thorough understanding of culture—what really motivates people's behaviors, attitudes, beliefs, and habits—will allow you, and any family members with you, to adapt with ease to both the social and business environment of China.

This book was developed to be easy, practical, and comprehensive. You'll first get your bearings on some general background information about China, such as its history, geography, political system, and social structure. This is no history text, though. The Background section is meant to be a brief survey that will familiarize you with some important landmarks you'll no doubt hear about or see. If something strikes you as interesting, the Background section will also serve you well as a way to get your feet wet in a particular area; we leave any further exploration of Chinese history up to you.

Next you'll read an overview of Chinese culture. For our purposes here, we've broken culture down into the following six categories: time, communication, group dynamics, status & hierarchy, relationships, and reasoning. Naturally, this provides only a general picture of the components of Chinese culture, but a very practical picture, too. And even while using these generalizations, we must never forget that any culture is made of individuals, and individuals vary. Learning about these important general concepts, though, where differences and pitfalls abound, will better prepare you and your family for a more successful experience abroad.

The following section, Living Abroad, is meant to give you some insight about the issues that people face in other cultures. Here you'll learn what to expect as a businessperson, a family member, a parent, a child, an individual, or a teenager. This section applies to life in any other culture, and you'll find the insight invaluable. It will raise the kind of important questions you'll want to consider when preparing to make an adjustment to life abroad. Most importantly, it will prepare you to face some tough challenges, and then reap some wonderful benefits.

The following two sections of the book, Getting Around in China and Living and Staying in China, are a comprehensive, step-by-step guide to everyday life in China. These are the issues that everyone must deal with, from driving and taking buses to shopping to waiting in line, to social etiquette. These sections are full of easily organized information, practical lists, and essential tips. Everyone—single traveler, parent, or child—will benefit.

Next are two sections designed specifically for the businessperson. In Business Environment, you'll get an idea of the general principles that govern working in China, from company values and structure, to chain of command, unions, work space, and women in business. Then, in Business Step-by-Step, you'll learn about the real essentials of doing business in China, ranging from such important issues as dress, speeches and presentations, and negotiations, to such often overlooked but crucial details as business card etiquette and making appointments.

Finally, we leave you with an introduction to the essentials of the Chinese language. While it is true that English is usually the lingua franca of global business, it cannot be denied that even a very basic knowledge of a foreign language can make a world of difference. This is no full-service Chinese language course; you won't be memorizing particles or complements. But you'll find that the minimal amount of time it takes to learn some basic social expressions and survival vocabulary will be recouped a hundred times over. Your Chinese colleagues and friends will be very appreciative that you've made an effort to learn just a little of their language. You'll find that the experience of another language is often its own reward, and you may even want to go further and learn to speak Chinese more fluently.

Good luck!, (or *Zhù nǐ hǎo yùn!*) and enjoy. We hope you find this course informative, practical, and enriching.

ONE

BACKGROUND

China is perhaps one of the most challenging cultures for a Westerner to understand. Doing business or living in China will challenge all of your assumptions about the way the world works. It often seems that the cultural gaps between East and West are unbridgeable. But this is especially true for China, since it spent so many years hidden behind the bamboo curtain. And when the curtain was pulled back, little information was available to outsiders about China.

Further adding to this confusion is the fact that the "traditional" Chinese culture is evolving as China enters the world market. China has gone from a traditional society based on Confucian ideals to the socialist mantle of communism to the current initiatives for a market economy within the space of a few generations. These transitions have created important differences between the older and younger generations as China opens to the world. Doing business requires a knowledge of both, as control remains largely in the hands of the elders. China, however, is poised on the cusp of change in the coming decades.

China remains an enigma even to those with years of experience within its borders. Just when you think you have a handle on the ways of the Chinese, someone invariably surprises you, challenging you to rethink everything you have learned about China. While a book such as this can attempt to point out common threads woven through Chinese culture, it certainly cannot dictate individual actions. However, as an old adage says, forewarned is forearmed. Knowing as much as possible about China and Chinese people can only help you achieve success in China.

As you work, live, and travel in China, the most important thing to remember is that, although Chinese want Western and American technology and goods, and although they may admire some parts of the American culture, they have no desire to *be* Americans. This is often something we often overlook, unable to see past China's recent history and, to be frank, in our eagerness to take advantage of all China has to offer. China, however, has a very long and distinguished history, one that Chinese are quite understandably proud of. The most successful foreigners in China seek to understand the Chinese culture and respect cultural differences.

Let's start with the basics.

VITAL STATISTICS

Official Name:	*Zhōnghuá Rénmín Gònghéguó* (People's Republic of China)
Capital:	Beijing

Flag:	Red with a large yellow five-pointed star and four smaller yellow five-pointed stars arranged in a vertical arc toward the middle of the flag
Area:	3,695,500 sq m
Land Distribution:	land 9,326,410 sq km; water 270,550 sq km; 10% arable land, 0% permanent crops, 43% permanent pastures, 15% forest and woodland, 33% other
Highest Point:	8,850 m (Mount Everest)
Lowest Point:	-154 m (Turpan Pendi)
Natural Resources:	coal, iron ore, petroleum, mercury, tin, tungsten, antimony, manganese, and more
Population (2002):	1,284,303,705
Population Growth (2002):	.87%
Urban/Rural Distribution:	37% urban
Largest Cities:	Beijing, Shanghai, Guangzhou
Ethnicity:	91.9% Han Chinese, 8.1% other
Language:	Mandarin[1], Yue (Cantonese), Wu (Shanghaiese), Minbei (Fuzhou), Minnan (Hokkien-Taiwanese), Xiang, Gan, Hakka dialects, and other minority languages
Literacy:	81.5%
Religions:	Officially atheist; Taoism, Buddhism, Islam, Christianity

[1] "Mandarin" is used by the outside world when referring to the Chinese language, while Chinese call it pǔtōng huà (standard Chinese) and the Taiwanese call it guó yǔ (language of the country).

Currency:	Chinese currency is called *rénmínbì* (literally "the people's money"); the unit of currency is the *yuán*, which equals 100 *fēn*. (Note: *rénmínbì* cannot be purchased outside of the PRC.)
GDP (2001):	$4,300 per capita
Major Trading Partners:	Hong Kong, U.S., Japan, South Korea, Germany, the Netherlands
Inflation (2001):	0.8%
Employment by Industry:	53% agriculture and forestry, 26% industry and commerce, 7% construction and mining, 4% social services, 10% other

For the most recent figures, please visit www.odci.gov/cia/publications/factbook/index.html

CLIMATE

In such a large country many diverse climates are inevitable. They range from subtropical and humid in the south to subarctic and arid in the north. Across China, January is the coldest month, ranging from 5°F (-15°C) in the north to 46°F (8°C) in the south. July and August are wet months, with monsoons battering the coastal regions.

PEOPLE

China boasts fifty-six different ethnic groups. The largest by far, comprising 91.9% of the total population, are Han Chinese. The remaining 8.1% is comprised of the following ethnic minorities: Achang, Bai, Blang, Bonan, Bouyei, Dai, Daur, Deang, Dong,

Dongxiang, Drung, Ewenki, Gaoshan, Gelo, Hani, Hezhen, Hui, Jing, Jingpo, Jino, Kazakh, Kirghiz, Korean, Lahu, Lhoba, Li, Lisu, Manchu, Maonan, Miao, Moinba, Mongolian, Mulam, Naxi, Nu, Oroqen, Ozbek, Pumi, Qiang, Russian, Salar, She, Shui, Tajik, Tatar, Tibetan, Tu, Tujia, Uygur, Va, Xibe, Yao, Yi, Yugur, and Zhuang. Of these, Zhuang, Manchu, and Hui are the largest; Lhoba, with a population of only 2,312 in the 1982 census, is the smallest.

China's ethnic minority groups are found largely in the border regions. Han, Hui, and Manchu all use the Han Chinese language; the others have a spoken language of their own, and twenty-three have a written language.

Many of the minority groups have retained distinctive ethnic clothing along with their language. You can distinguish Tibetans by their robes, Uygurs by their embroidered skullcaps, Yi by their *cha'erwa* (woolen cloaks) and Mongolians by their robes and riding boots. Similarly, you will encounter different types of cuisine and housing, from the usual courtyard dwellings to tent-like yurts in the north and balustrade-style *ganfan* houses in the south, as you travel around the country.

By the Way...

OVERSEAS CHINESE

One can be Chinese anywhere in the world. The term "overseas Chinese" refers to anyone of Chinese origin who lives abroad, regardless of citizenship or place of birth. This group is very important to China, both politically and economically. Overseas Chinese have provided business contacts and financial support, both of which have put or kept government officials in power. In addition, the majority of foreign investment in China is from overseas Chinese.

CHINESE HISTORY IN BRIEF

China has a legitimate claim to one of the longest, if not the longest, continuous histories among modern countries. Here are the broad strokes of this rich civilization.

THE DYNASTIES

C.2200 BC–C.1750 BC	**Xia Dynasty. Recent archeological findings have proven this myth a reality. This first (known) Chinese dynasty is thought to be descended from a Yellow River Valley neolithic culture. Evidence suggests that the Xia had a developed writing system.**
C.1750 BC–C.1040 BC	**Shang Dynasty. Probably characterized by the oldest bronze-working people, the Shang Dynasty was a slave society given to human sacrifice. This dynasty provides the oldest known record of Chinese writing.**
C.1100 BC–771 BC	**Western Zhou Dynasty. In a China comprised of many quasi-independent principalities, the Zhou were the most powerful family and ruled the area as a hegemony. Located in the center of the principalities, they gave the name "the Middle Kingdom" to China.**
770 BC–256 BC	**Eastern Zhou Dynasty. Following the conquest of the Zhou capital by barbarians from the west, the Zhou moved east, but their power inevitably declined.**
722 BC–481 BC	**Spring and Autumn Period. Named after the book "The Spring and Autumn Annals," which recorded the history of**

the period, this golden age of China saw the birth of new philosophies and new ideas, including Taoism and Confucianism.

403 BC–221 BC   Warring States Period. Although war was not unfamiliar to earlier periods, in this era war metamorphosed from one-day battles between small armies to long battles and sieges between armies of half a million soldiers.

221 BC–206 BC   Qin Dynasty. Qin Shihuangdi, the first Emperor of China (earlier rulers were kings), conquered and united China. Among his accomplishments in his tenure as emperor was the linking of the packed-earth defensive walls of the former principalities into the Great Wall of China (although the Wall as it stands today was constructed some 2,000 years later during the Ming dynasty). The Qin dynasty saw the beginning of an imperial system of administration that served as the pattern for dynasties over the next two millennia.

206 BC–AD 8   Earlier Han Dynasty. Today's majority ethnic Han population was named for this dynasty. Han rulers modified the imperial systems put in place by Qin, most notably by tempering the draconian approach to government to one based on Confucian ideals. Intellectual, artistic, and literary arts were revived and prospered. During this period, "silk routes" to Antioch, Baghdad, and Alexandria were established and parts of Vietnam and Korea were invaded and annexed.

AD 8–AD 24	Interim Period. As the result of a power struggle within the royal family, Wang Mang, a member of the royal household, although a commoner, was appointed emperor.
AD 25–220	Eastern Han Dynasty. Following the death of Wang Mang, the imperial throne was taken back by the Hans. Over the next two centuries, the dynasty gradually declined and, finally, rife with corruption, collapsed.
220–265	Three Kingdoms. The collapse of the Han dynasty ushered in four centuries of rule by warlords. Three kingdoms, Wei, Shu, and Wu, had overlapping reigns during this period. Buddhism, introduced during the Han dynasty, began to take root in China.
265–420	Jin Dynasty. China once again saw unity, but the Jin were unable to withstand the invasions of nomadic people and were forced to relocate their capital from Luoyang in the north to Nanjing in the south.
420–589	Southern and Northern Dynasties.
581–618	Sui Dynasty. Although short-lived, this dynasty saw the reunification of China under a brutal tyranny that included crushing taxes and forced labor on the Grand Canal and the reconstruction of the Great Wall.
618–907	Tang Dynasty. During the Tang dynasty, regarded as one of the greatest in China's history, China's territory was expanded and a golden age of literature and the arts arrived.

907–960	Five Dynasties. Following the decline of the Tang dynasty, China was fragmented into five northern dynasties and ten southern kingdoms.
960–1127	Northern Song Dynasty. Most of China was again reunified under the Song dynasty. Bureaucracy was centralized, and burgeoning centers of trade and industry were developed. The mercantile class gained wealth and prestige.
1127–1279	Southern Song Dynasty. The Song dynasty was forced to flee the north in the face of nomadic invasions.
1206–1368	Yuan (Mongol) Dynasty. Established by Mongol Kublai Khan, the Yuan dynasty was the first non-Chinese dynasty to rule China. The Yuan brought back

Confucian ideals in an attempt to impose order on the Chinese people. Cultural achievements flourished as China had its first major encounters with West Asia and Europe. The first recorded visits by Westerners, including Marco Polo, occurred during this period.

1368–1644   Ming Dynasty. Founded by a Han Chinese peasant and former Buddhist monk turned rebel army leader, the Neo-Confucian Ming bureaucracy reinstated an agrarian-centered society, rein-forcing an isolationist ideal that things foreign were neither necessary nor welcome. During this period, the Great Wall was fortified (to its current state, not counting repairs) and the Forbidden City was built.

1644–1911   Qing (Manchu) Dynasty. After long wars with the Mongols weakened the Ming dynasty, the Manchu invaded, taking Beijing and establishing the last imperial dynasty, China's second foreign rule. The Manchu strategy was to allow for the continuation of the Han ways of government, although the highest positions were always held by the Manchu, not the Han. However, the Manchu were not interested in being integrated with the Han; the Han were not permitted to emigrate to the Manchu homelands, and intermarriage between Manchu and Han was forbidden. During this period, the Manchu conquered Mongolia and Central Asia, freeing China from the threat of invasion by land for the first time. Taiwan was incorporated into China.

Along with the rest of Asia, China began to have contact with the West in the 17th and 18th centuries, leading to the expansion of existing trade routes further west and into Europe. However, while there was demand in Europe and America for tea, silk, and porcelain, China didn't need Western goods, which created trade imbalances, especially for the British. To compensate, the British began trading goods from India, mostly cotton and opium. This was in spite of an imperial ban on opium.

1839–42   The Opium War. The Qing government suppresses illegal opium traffic and destroys large quantities of British opium in an attempt to free large numbers of the population from the purposeful enslavement to opium imposed by the British. The British retaliate, initiating the Opium War. Britain defeats China, and China is forced to sign the vastly unfair Treaty of Nanjing, with concessions including the ceding of Hong Kong to Britain.

1851–64   The Taiping Rebellion. Hong Xiuquan leads an uprising in Guizhou Province, taking Nanjing and proclaiming the Heavenly Kingdom of Great Peace, with himself as king. Over 30 million people were killed before the Chinese army succeeded in crushing the revolt.

1898   The Hundred Days' Reform. The Qing emperor Guangxu launches a series of sweeping social and institutional reforms called the Hundred Days' Reform, which ended when the Empress Dowager Ci Xi and her ultraconservative supporters engineered a coup d'etat and rescinded the edicts.

MODERN CHINA EMERGES

1911	The Qing dynasty falls, ending over three millennia of Chinese dynastic rule.
1912	The Republic of China is founded with Dr. Sun Yat-sen as president.
1919	During World War I, Japan seizes German holdings in Shandong Province; China protests, but in 1918 the Chinese government agrees to accept Japan's claim on the area. The people react to the sellout with public outcry; on May 4, 1919, student demonstrations mark the beginning of the May Fourth Movement.
1937	Beginning of war with Japan.
1934–35	Mao Ze-dong's Long March saves the Communists from defeat at the hands of Chiang Kai-shek.
1946–49	Civil war between the Nationalists and the Communists. Following the defeat of the Nationalists, the Communists establish the People's Republic of China with Mao Ze-dong at the helm on Oct. 1, 1949.
1948–49	China is one of the original twenty-three signatories of the General Agreement on Tariffs and Trade (GATT); however, in 1949, following the revolution, the government in Taiwan withdraws from the agreement.
1953	First Five-Year Plan for economic development is instituted.
1958	The Great Leap Forward, a campaign by Mao Ze-dong to increase industrial and agricultural production in order to catch up with more advanced countries; the goals were national self-sufficiency, collectivization, and labor-intensive methods.

1963	China severs ties with the Soviet Union, which it believes has lost sight of true communist principles.
1966–76	The Great Proletarian Cultural Revolution, a political campaign to rekindle revolutionary fervor.
1972	China receives United States president Richard Nixon
1976	Deaths of Mao Ze-dong and Zhou En-lai, China's premier.
1977	Deng Xiaoping becomes deputy prime minister and begins economic reform.
1979	China and the United States establish diplomatic relations.
1986	China applies to resume its status as a GATT Contracting Party; a Working Party is formed to examine the issue in 1987.
1989	Pro-democratic student demonstrations in Tiananmen Square.
1995	Sino-American relationship becomes strained when President Clinton allows Taiwan's president to visit the United States. The Working Party established to examine China's role in GATT is converted to a WTO Working Party when GATT is replaced by the World Trade Organization.
1997	Deng Xiaoping dies; Hong Kong reverts to China as a special administrative region.
1999	The U.S. government issues a report accusing China of espionage, beginning in 1970, to acquire information on the design of thermonuclear weapons.
1999	Sino-American relations suffer further strain when the United States bombs the Chinese

embassy in Belgrade as part of a NATO strike against Serb military installations. The United States claims that the bombing was a mistake.

2000   China and the United States continue to work toward trade agreements despite disagreements over Taiwan, human rights issues, the NATO bombing, and lingering charges of espionage.

NOTED (AND NOTORIOUS) CHINESE

In Politics

SHI HUANG-DI (256 BC–210 BC)

The first emperor of China, Shi Huang-di (more commonly known as *Qin Shihuang* in China) conquered the states of Han, Zhao, Wei, Chu, Yan and Qi. He not only consolidated the Chinese regions into a single state, he also imposed uniformity; maintaining local forms of currency, weights and measures, or writing scripts became an act of treason.

PU YI (1906–1967)

China's last emperor, Pu Yi was only three years old when he was named emperor. When he was five, rebellion swept through the country as resentment against foreigners and the Manchu government grew, and Pu Yi was forced to abdicate. He continued to live in the Forbidden City and was treated with great respect. When he was nine, a warlord named Chang Hsun restored Pu Yi to the throne, a return that lasted only days. In 1931, the Japanese invaded Manchuria and installed Pu Yi as the chief executive, a puppet position. Following World War II, the Soviets invaded Manchuria and Pu Yi was kept in the USSR under house arrest. He was returned to China in 1950, and he was consigned to a prison camp there. After nine years of labor, he was released, but remained under the control of the Chinese communist government until his death.

SUN YAT-SEN (1866–1925)

Also known as *Sūn Zhōng-shān* and *Sūn Wén*, Sun Yat-sen gave up his medical career to dedicate himself to overthrowing the weak and corrupt Manchu dynasty and establishing a republic. In 1894, Sun established the revolutionary *Xīng Zhōng Hùi* (Society for Regenerating China) in Honolulu, Hawaii, with a group of overseas Chinese youths. He developed the Three Principles of the People—nationalism, democracy, and social well-being—as the guidelines for modernizing China. After many years and many armed attacks, Sun's people at last took Wuchang, the capital of Hupei Province, and urged the Chinese people to rise up against the imperial government. Sun's uprising led to the dissolution of the 5,000-year-old Chinese monarchy, and the return of China to the common people.

MAO ZE-DONG (1893–1976)

One of the founders of the Chinese Communist Party in 1921, Mao Ze-dong founded the People's Republic of China in 1949 and was its head of state until 1959. Even after that tenure, he continued to pull the strings of government until his death in 1976. A Marxist thinker, Mao unified the country and led the greatest social revolution in China. His revolution included the collectivization of land and property, the weakening of the urban bourgeoisie, and the granting of status to peasants and workers.

ZHOU EN-LAI (1898–1976)

A Chinese diplomat, Zhou En-lai was the premier of China from 1949 to 1976. His historic meeting with U.S. president Richard Nixon marked a turning point in Sino-U.S. relations.

DENG XIAOPING (1904–1997)

Once the Secretary General of the Chinese Communist Party, Deng Xiaoping, was removed from office during Mao Ze-dong's Great Leap

Forward. He returned to power in 1974, having been "rehabilitated," and remained the de facto leader of China until his death. Deng Xiaoping instituted the Four Modernizations of agriculture, industry, technology and defense, along with the Four Cardinal Principles. He also put in motion the dismantling of collectivism and rejected Máo's ideals of self-sufficiency for more openness to foreign investment. His policies set off an economic boom which led to a tripling of average incomes in the early 1990s, easing the extreme poverty of many Chinese.

In Arts & Literature

LI BAI (701–762)

The Tang dynasty produced many of China's greatest poets, including LiBai, who contributed enormously to the Chinese literary culture. A Taoist and bohemian, Li's poetry reflects his volatile, larger-than-life temperament.

SU DONGPO (1037–1101)

Su was a talented calligrapher, painter, and poet, as well as an outspoken policy critic. His poetry encompasses an exceptional variety of subjects and careful attention to detail, invoking a visual impression. Some 800 letters and over 2,700 poems by Su Dongpo have survived the centuries.

LU XUN (1881–1936)

Lu Xun is known as the founding father of modern Chinese literature. His stories, poetry and essays reflected the lives of Chinese people in the early 20th century. His novel, *Kuáng Rén Rì Jì* (*A Madman's Diary*), is widely acknowledged as the first story to be written in the modern folk Chinese language.

ZHANG YIMOU (1950–)

One of the leading directors of China's "Fifth Generation" filmmakers, Zhang Yimou made his directorial debut in 1987 with *Hóng Gāo Liáng* (*Red Sorghum*), for which he won China's first

Golden Bear award at the 1988 Berlin Festival. Earlier in his life, Zhang Yimou received the Best Actor award from the Tokyo Film Festival for his performance in *Lǎo Jǐng* (*The Old Well*).

In Philosophy & Science

LAO TZU (BORN C. 600 BC)

Known as the "Old Master," Lao Tzu wrote the principles of Taoism in the Tao-Te Ching. He believed that simplicity is the key to freedom and happiness and that a true life is a life that conforms to the laws of nature rather than the laws of man.

CONFUCIUS (551 BC–479 BC)

Confucius, originally Kong Qiu and better known as Kongfuzi or Kongzi in China, whether via his own word or those of his followers, is the source of much of the foundation of China. He advocated traditional roles and hierarchies that would lead to moral behavior. For more on his philosophy, see the section on Confucianism in the Culture section.

YANG CHEN-NING (1922–)

Yang Chen-ning, together with Tsung Dao Lee, won the 1957 Nobel Prize in Physics for their research on parity laws. Their work has led to important discoveries regarding the elementary particles.

GOVERNMENT & POLITICS

The People's Republic of China consists of twenty-three *sheng* (provinces), five *zìzhìqū* (autonomous regions), and four *zhí xià shì* (municipalities). China also has a policy of regional autonomy for various ethnic groups; in addition to the provinces, autonomous regions, and municipalities listed below, China has 30 autonomous prefectures and 124 autonomous counties.

BACKGROUND

PROVINCES	CAPITAL CITY
Ānhuī	Héféi
Fújiàn	Fúzhōu
Gānsū	Lánzhōu
Guǎngdōng	Guǎngzhōu
Guìzhōu	Guìyáng
Hǎinán	Hǎikǒu
Héběi	Shíjiāzhuāng
Hēilóngjiāng	Hārbīn
Hénán	Zhèngzhōu
Húběi	Wǔhàn
Húnán	Chángshā
Jiāngsū	Nánjīng
Jiāngxī	Nánchāng
Jílín	Chángchūn
Liáoníng	Shěnyáng
Qīnghǎi	Xīníng
Shǎnxī	Xī'ān
Shāndōng	Jìnán
Shānxī	Tàiyuán
Sìchuān (Szechwan)	Chéngdū
Táiwān[2]	Táiběi
Yúnnán	Kūnmíng
Zhèjiang	Hángzhōu

[2] Although Taiwan considers itself the seat of government for the island of Taiwan and all territories of maninland China, including what is now independent Mongolia, the PRC considers Taiwan a province. Hong Kong is a special administrative region.

AUTONOMOUS REGIONS	CAPITAL CITY
Guǎngxī Zhuàngzú zìzhì qū	Nánnáng
Nèi Měng Gǔ (Inner Mongolia)	Hūhéhaòtè

Níngxià Huízú zìzhì qū	Yínchuān
Xīnjiāng	
Wéiwúěrzìzhì qū	Wūlǔmùqí
Xīzàng (Tibet)	Lāsà

MUNICIPALITIES

Běijīng
Chóngqìng
Shànghǎi
Tiānjīn

China and Taiwan

The histories of mainland China and Taiwan are inextricably inter-twined. Taiwan is a province of China and its population is a com-bination of aboriginals and emigrees. Taiwan was a Japanese colony for many years during the first decades of the 20th century, but returned to Chinese control in 1945, following Japan's defeat in World War II. When Mao Ze-dong came into power just four years later and installed a communist government, the leaders of the for-mer nationalist government fled to Taiwan and set up a govern-ment-in-exile. Both Beijing and Taipei claim leadership of the Chinese people, Beijing calling the country the People's Republic of China and Taipei calling it the Republic of China. The current sta-tus of the conflict is largely that of a deferred civil war. The United States began normalizing relations with mainland China in 1972 with President Nixon's visit. This relationship was strained, howev-er, in 1995 when President Clinton allowed Taiwan's president, Lee Teng-hui, to visit the United States. Taiwan's election of a pro-sepa-ratist president in 2000 worsened these tensions.

It is worth noting, however, that despite the conflict, mainland China and Taiwan have been doing business with each other for over two decades to the economic benefit of both, and restrictions have been lifted, allowing many Taiwanese to travel to the mainland to visit their ancestral lands.

China's Government

China is governed by the State Council, which is appointed by the National People's Congress (NPC) and is accountable to it. The president and vice president are elected by the NPC for five-year terms; the premier is nominated by the president and confirmed by the NPC.

The legislative branch of Chinese government is the unicameral *Quánguó Rénmín Dàibĭao Dàhuì* or National People's Congress (NPC). NPC members are elected by regional and municipal people's congresses for five year terms. Judicial functions are carried out by the Supreme People's Court, whose judges are appointed by the NPC.

The Chinese Communist Party (CCP)

China essentially has only one party: the Chinese Communist Party (CCP). Although there are eight other registered parties, all of them are small, and all are controlled by the CCP. Until recently it was virtually impossible to distinguish between the party and the government—the policies of the government were those of the party. In recent years, however, a move has begun to shift policy making to the CCP and policy implementation to the government.

The Democratic Parties

The largest of the democratic parties, the Chinese Democratic League, was founded in 1941 and has around 120,000 members. It is comprised largely of intellectuals.

The China Democratic National Construction Association was founded in 1945. Its 61,000 members are largely economic scholars and experts.

The Jĭu Sān Society, founded in 1944, has approximately 57,000 members, mostly in the fields of science, technology, education, and medicine.

Founded in 1945, the China Association for Promoting Democracy has about 56,000 members, largely educators and intellectuals.

The 55,000 members of the Chinese Peasants' and Workers' Democratic Party, started in 1930, are mostly found in the fields of health, education, science, and technology.

The China Revolutionary Committee of Kuomintang was founded in 1948 and has almost 50,000 members, most of whom have historical ties with the Kuomintang.

China Zhi Gong Dang, founded in 1925, has approximately 13,000 members. The party consists largely of overseas Chinese who have returned to China and other individuals with overseas connections.

The smallest of the democratic parties, the Taiwan Democratic Self-Government League has a mere 1,400 members, mostly individuals who are from Taiwan or who have family ties there.

RELIGION

Although China is officially atheist, it has historically adopted a pragmatic and eclectic attitude toward belief systems, and it has incorporated Taoism, Buddhism, Islam, and Christianity into its societal fabric. Indeed, the typical Chinese philosophy is a rich tapestry of Confucianism, Taoism, and Buddhism. In theory, Chinese have the freedom of religious belief, and their religious activities are protected by China's constitution. However, there are only two government-sanctioned sects of Christianity—the Catholic church without ties to Rome and the "Three-Self-Patriotic" Protestant church. Other "unauthorized" churches exist in many parts of China, where the local governments may tolerate them, attempt outright to control them, or offer them treatment that falls somewhere between the two.

Because of the hodgepodge of beliefs, it is difficult to pigeonhole people as belonging to any one religion. However, official figures put Buddhism in the forefront, with an estimated 100 million adherents. Traditional Taoism also is practiced. Official figures indicate there are 18 million Muslims, 10 million Protestants, and 4 million Catholics; unofficial estimates are much higher.

Religion often follows ethnic divisions. Hui, Uygur, Kazakh, Kirghiz, Tatar, Ozbek, Tajik, Dongxiang, Salar, and Bonan, for example, follow Islam. Tibetans, Mongolians, Lhobas, Moinbas, Tus, and Yugurs subscribe to Lamaism (Tibetan Buddhism), while Dai, Blang, and Deang are largely Hinayana Buddhist. Many Miao, Yao, and Yi are Catholic or Protestant; Han are mainly divided among Buddhism, Protestantism, Catholicism, or Taoism.

Taoism

Taoism developed from a philosophy based upon the writings of Lao Tzu, a contemporary of Confucius in the 1st century BC. Taking form in the 2nd century, Taoism is one of two belief systems indigenous to China. Lao Tze and his followers emphasized individual freedom, laissez-faire government, human spontaneity, and mystical experience. The goal of Taoism is to attain balance and harmony with nature and spiritual forces, as well as within oneself. *Tao*, the Way, is the journey to understanding the unseen reality behind appearances.

Confucianism

Confucianism, the other indigenous Chinese belief system, provided a large part of the foundation of the Chinese society and culture. It is discussed in greater detail in the chapter on Culture.

Buddhism

Buddhism was begun in India by Siddhārtha Gautama, a prince turned teacher and philosopher. The name Buddha means "enlightened." The ideals of Buddhism focus on achieving freedom from the cycle of death and rebirth and thereby entering into Nirvana, perfect and total peace and enlightenment.

The centerpiece of Buddhism is the Four Noble Truths:

- Life is suffering.
- Desire is the cause of suffering.
- When you cease to desire, you eliminate suffering.
- Desire, and thus suffering, can be eliminated by following the Middle Way and the Eightfold Noble Path.

The Middle Way is exactly that: a way of life that exists between the wanton sating of desire and zealous self-denial. The Eightfold Noble Truths consist of right views, intention, speech, conduct, livelihood, effort, attention, and meditation.

Buddhism reached China via foreign merchants on the trade routes to the west. By AD 166, Buddhism had a presence in the imperial court, although it remained primarily a religion practiced by foreigners until the beginning of the 4th century. By the end of the 5th century, it had swept across China. In Tibet, Buddhism evolved into Lamaism, also known as Tibetan Buddhism.

Islam

China was introduced to Islam by Arab and Persian merchants, probably during the 8th century. The Muslim god is Allah, and their prophet is Muhammad, who was born in Mecca around AD 570. The revelations of Muhammad were compiled in the Koran, which sets forth the four principal tenets of Islam:

- Faith in the absolute unity of Allah
- Belief in angels as messengers of Allah
- Belief in prophetic messengers (Muhammed being the last of these, following Jesus and the Old Testament prophets)
- Belief in a final judgment which will reward the faithful

Salvation is achieved through the Five Acts of Worship, or the Pillars of Islam:

- Physical and spiritual purification
- Prayer

- Giving of alms
- Fasting during the holy month of Ramadan
- The hajj, or pilgrimage to Mecca

By the Way...

WHO GOES THERE?

As you travel around China, you may notice pictures or statues at the entrances of homes, temples, and shops. These are probably the door gods, who ward off evil spirits. Traditionally, Shin Shu and Yu Lei (also known as Ch'in Shu-pao and Hu Ching-te) were guards assigned to the entrance of the Door of the Spirits, through which all souls pass after death. Over the years they evolved into the guardians of the home.

In keeping with the Chinese tradition of mixing and matching religions and philosophical beliefs, Chinese folk religions are woven throughout the land. Shen Shu and Yu Lei guard doors. Likewise, Tsao Chun, the Kitchen God, may watch over the family from his place above the kitchen stove. Images of these gods and others, such as the Gods of Happiness, Wealth, and Longevity and the God of Literature are scattered throughout China's culture.

HOLIDAYS & FESTIVALS

PUBLIC HOLIDAYS IN CHINA

In addition to its ten public holidays, China boasts any number of national, regional and local holidays. In fact, almost every village has its own traditional folk festival. Along the coast and along the rivers, annual dragon boat races are popular events, sure to elicit a large turnout with much shouting and excitement as everyone roots for a team of rowers.

January 1	Xīn Nián	New Year
January/February³	Chūn Jié	Spring Festival (the lunar New Year)
March 8	Guó Jì Láo Dòng Fù Nǚ Jié	International Women's Day
May 1	Guó Jì Láo Dòng Jié	International Labor Day
May 4	Wǔ Sì Qīng Nián Jié	Chinese Youth Day
June 1	Guó Jì ér Tóng Jié	International Children's Day
August 1	Jiàn Jūn Jié	Army Day
September 10	Jiào Shī Jié	Teachers' Day
October 1	Guó Qìng Jié	National Day

³ Movable according to the lunar calendar; falls on the first day of the lunar new year.

Chūn Jié
(Spring Festival/Lunar New Year)

At the beginning of spring, Chinese exuberantly celebrate the first traditional festival of the year, the Spring Festival or Lunar New Year. Each household is decorated with Spring Festival pictures and verses. Spring Festival Eve is a time for family reunions, when the entire family gets together for a New Year's Eve dinner, followed by game playing and conversation until the wee hours of the morning. On the morning of the new year, people call on relatives and friends. Festivities during the Spring Festival include the traditional lion dance, dragon-lantern dance, fireworks, and stilt-walking. During the Spring Festival, China effectively shuts down as people celebrate the new year.

Yuán Xiāo Jié (Lantern Festival)

Closely following *Chūn Jié* is *Yuán Xiāo Jié*, the Lantern Festival (also a day of remembrance), taking place on the first full moon after the Spring Festival. The tradition of displaying lanterns on this day dates back to the 1st century. Today many cities hold lantern fairs to display many exotic and wondrous multicolored lanterns. In rural areas, people gather together to witness fireworks, stilt walking, dragon lantern performances, and to dance the *yaggee* and other folk dances.

All over the country people eat a special sweet dumpling called *yuánxiāo*, round balls of glutinous rice flour stuffed with sugar or bean fillings, symbolizing reunion.

Qīng Míng Jié (Pure Brightness Day)

Qīng Míng Jié comes around April 5 every year. Originally a day to offer sacrifices to one's ancestors, today Chinese visit the tombs of the martyrs of the revolution to pay their respects. They also gather with friends to enjoy the arrival of spring, walk, and fly kites. City dwellers flock to the outskirts of town for the pleasure of feeling the newly green grass beneath their feet. For this reason, Pure Brightness Day is sometimes also called the "Stepping on Greenery Festival."

Duān Wǔ Jié (Dragon Boat Festival)

Duān Wǔ Jié, the Dragon Boat Festival, falls on the fifth day of the fifth lunar month. The Dragon Boat Festival celebrates the memory of the ancient patriotic poet Qu Yuan, a native of the state of Chu during the Warring States Period. Qu Yuan tried repeatedly to help his king eliminate rampant political corruption. Finally, slandered by malicious court officials, he was sent into exile by the king. In 278 BC, when the capital of Chu was conquered by the State of Qin, Qu Yuan drowned himself in despair on the fifth day of the fifth lunar month. The people who lived by the river set out in their boats to try to find his body, but they could not. Every year on the anniversary of his death, people row dragon boats on their local rivers in memory of Qu Yuan's life and death, throwing sections of bamboo filled with rice into the river as an offering. Legend says that someone once met Qu Yuan's spirit on the bank of the river. Qu Yuan said that the food the people had given him was taken away by a dragon. He asked that the rice be wrapped in bamboo leaves and tied with five-colored thread, the two things that the dragon is most afraid of. Today, *zòngzi*—rice wrapped in a pyramid shape with bamboo or reed leaves—is the traditional food for the Dragon Boat Festival, and is still eaten in memory of Zòngzi.

Zhōng Qiū Jié (Mid-Autumn Festival)

On the day of the exact middle of autumn, the fifteenth day of the eighth lunar month, Chinese celebrate *Zhōng Qiū Jié*, the Mid-Autumn Festival. *Zhōng Qiū Jié* originated with people offering elaborate cakes to the moon spirit on this day. Today the festival revolves around a reunion of family. Because the moon is full and especially bright, families sit together under the moonlight eating "moon cakes." Those who are away from home during the Mid-Autumn Festival might recall the words of the great Tang Dynasty poet Li Bai: "I raise my head to gaze at the bright moon, and I drop my head to think of my old home."

Other Festivals and Celebrations

Across the country, ethnic minority groups have retained their own traditional festivals. Among these are the:

- Water Splashing Festival of the Dai people
- Nadam Fair of the Mongolian people
- Torch Festival of the Yi people
- Danu (Never Forget the Past) Festival of the Yao people
- Third Month Fair of the Bai people
- Antiphonal Singing Day of the Zhuang people
- Tibetan New Year and Onghor (Expecting Good Harvest) Festival of the Tibetan people.

EDUCATIONAL SYSTEM

Chinese children attend school for a minimum of nine years, courtesy of the Law on Nine-Year Compulsory Education, which took effect on July 1, 1986. The measures put in place by this law were designed to bring the educational programs of rural areas, which often had only four to six years of compulsory education, up to par with urban schools. The overriding goal was to modernize the school system in order to produce graduates who would be skilled in all trades and professions and able to help China meet its challenges.

While the government has authority over the educational system, the Chinese Communist Party plays a significant role in the system through school administrators who are party members and who are relied on to ensure that education reflects the mandates of the party.

Preschool Education

Parents can enroll their children in preschool at age three and a half. Preschools are part of the welfare services of the government, but also depend on the sponsorship of individual organizations.

Primary Education

At age seven, children are enrolled in primary school, which takes place six days a week, with a long vacation in July and August. There is some difference in the school schedules of rural areas, which tend to have more flexible half-day schedules instead of full days. Primary education in most areas is five years, except in cities such as Beijing and Shanghai, where it is six years. The curriculum consists of Chinese, mathematics, physical education, arts, sciences, and foreign languages, combined with practical work experience around the school compound from grade four onward. Political and moral training in communist ideology, love of country, and love of the party are typical parts of the curriculum. Although the enrollment percentage in primary schools is high, the dropout rates are equally high, with as much as 10% of the student population, mostly in rural areas, leaving school between each grade.

Secondary Education

Middle schools are divided into two levels: junior and senior. Junior middle school begins at age twelve and lasts three years. Senior middle school begins at age fifteen and adds another two or three years. The curriculum mirrors that of primary education, although some schools add vocational classes to the mix.

Because of the low number of compulsory education years, a person who has graduated from senior middle school is considered an educated person. Graduation from middle school means that one might be able to attend university, but in reality there are a limited number of spaces for higher education students, so most go directly from middle school into the work force.

Vocational and Technical Education

There are four different types of vocational and technical schools, some of which overlap with regular middle schools. Technical schools offer a four-year course following junior middle school and a further two to three years in fields such as commerce, legal occupations, and fine arts. Workers' training schools are available to graduates of senior middle school who have had at least two years of education in a trade, such as carpentry. Vocational technical middle schools accept either junior or senior middle school students for a course of study in service areas such as cooking and tailoring. And finally, agricultural middle schools offer a curriculum that includes agricultural science along with the standard subjects.

Post-secondary Education

Much has changed since the Cultural Revolution and the years thereafter. Reforms implemented in 1976 began to equalize enrollment for all children, taking focus away from the children of influential parents, where the main criterion was loyalty to the party, and adding it to a more diverse group of students selected on academic, rather than political, grounds.

Higher education consists of labor colleges, for training agrotechnicians, factory-run colleges, which provide technical education for workers, and universities.

CHINA—CULTURE

We all have programmed into us a certain code, a set of rules by which we live and interpret the world. These rules govern both our actions and our reactions. They are instilled in us by our parents, our teachers, and our peers. Culture, then, is the combined values, beliefs, mores, motivations and attitudes that shape our view of the world.

Though we are all individuals, we are all influenced by the culture in which we grow up. Despite our individual differences, there are nevertheless cultural ties that bind us together. No matter how little someone from Des Moines thinks he has in common with a New Yorker and vice versa, they are indeed more similar to each other than to someone from Tokyo or Riyadh.

This chapter explores the cultural differences between China and the United States. Although endless distinctions can be made between cultures, or individuals for that matter, here we break culture down into six different categories that will paint a practical picture and an accessible portrait of Chinese culture viewed through American eyes. These categories are: time, communication, group dynamics, status & hierarchy, relationships, and reasoning. Each section begins with a brief overview of the category and its polar opposites. As we explore the category in more depth, we will take a look at where China and the United States fall on the continuum and how they relate to each other. By the end of the section, you should have a greater understanding of what may cause cultural misunderstanding and an idea of the very real challenges communicating across cultures can present. Finally, we'll provide you with some tips to help you apply this information to daily interaction. We will use this knowledge later as we take a step-by-step look at the Chinese business culture.

With any luck, you will emerge with a better understanding not only of what makes China tick, but also of what makes *you* tick. Only when you are able to understand that cultural differences are neither bad nor good, merely different ways to look at the same reality, can you begin to build the cross-cultural skills you will need to be successful in China—or anywhere else in the world for that matter.

The following observations are of necessity painted in broad brush strokes. It is naturally unwise to think that every Chinese person will behave in one way, and every American in another. However, there is enough evidence to support the idea that the Chinese as a culture tend to have certain preferences, as do Americans. Keeping that in mind, the information in this chapter will give you a foundation on which to lay the bricks of individual characteristics, quirks, and foibles.

THE CONFUCIAN TRADITIONS
OF CHINA

China's cultural roots are deeply embedded in Confucianism. Confucius (Kong Qiu) was a philosopher who lived from 551 BC to 479 BC. His philosophies became the foundation upon which Chinese society was built and which sustained it for nearly 2,000 years, shaping the mores and behaviors of the Chinese. Confucius believed that moral behavior stemmed from the fulfillment of traditional roles and hierarchies. He defined five basic relationships, which he called *wu lun*. Each relationship represents a reciprocal obligation.

Emperor to Subject
An emperor must show his subjects kindness;
a subject must be loyal.

Father to Son
A father must provide protection and favor to his son; the son reciprocates with respect and obedience.

Husband to Wife
A husband has the obligation to provide for his wife; a wife respectfully submits.

Older Brother to Younger Brother
The older brother cares for his younger brother; the younger brother models himself after his older brother.

Friend to Friend
The relationship between friends is one of mutual trust.

The result of this system of interdependent relationships is a structure in which the lower level gives obedience to the higher level, a characteristic that extends from the family level to the national. From this basic framework come ideas of hierarchy, group orientation, and respect for age and tradition. And, although it may seem antithetical, it also creates a high regard for strict egalitarianism within each level of the hierarchy (albeit a different concept of egalitarianism than is generally held in the West, a concept discussed in later paragraphs). It's important to remember that the basis of this system is not the subjugation of one person by another. It is concern for one person by another. According to Confucian thought, when one's basic motivation is the well-being of another person, then one's behavior is moral.

THE YIN AND YANG OF CHINESE CULTURE

China is an enigma to many Westerners. Doing business in China can seem at times to be no different than doing business in the United States, at other times it is impossible to believe that the two cultures can work successfully together.

China today, especially in the business environment, might be likened to a lacquered box, a veneer of modernism overlaying an intricately carved history of tradition. Recent years have seen profound changes in China, both political and economic. China experienced the end of dynastic rule less than one hundred years ago, followed by communism, the Great Leap Forward, the Cultural Revolution, and modernization. China has gone from feudalism to collectivism to privatization in just one century.

In order to understand the China of today, you must understand the China of yesterday. Like the yin and yang symbol, the two sides are inextricably joined, together creating the country that is China. To the Chinese mind the ideas and values of the past and the present are not mutually exclusive. Just as they have blended the teachings of Confucianism, Taoism and Buddhism into a uniquely Chinese philosophy, so have they adapted and developed traditional values to create a modern China.

As we explore the different facets of culture, we will look at both sides of China, past and present.

TIME

*You can't buy an inch of time
with an inch of gold.*

—Chinese proverb

*Already a month behind schedule and the end wasn't even in sight.
When Chris Russell had begun looking for a Chinese supplier, his
goal was to locate a company, negotiate a contract, and have ship-
ments begin within the month. Now, two months later, they were in
the middle of negotiation, but Chris was beginning to suspect that*

they would not be receiving their goods for at least another month. Chris sighed in frustration—now there would be yet another meeting where Chris would have to try to explain why they weren't getting anywhere with the Chinese.

Rigid versus Flexible Cultures

Perhaps the first cultural challenge people encounter, often subconsciously, when they meet another culture is the difference in the perception of time. Time is a resource that different cultures view differently. We all have different answers to the questions "What is the value of time?" and "How is time best spent?" In the most basic terms, time can be either flexible or rigid.

In a rigid time culture, the clock is the measure against which all of our actions are judged: whether we are saving time or wasting it, whether we are on time or late. People in rigid time cultures like to plan their activities and keep a schedule. It is rude to show up late and important not to waste other people's time. Time is a commodity that must be spent wisely, not frittered away.

The clock for flexible time cultures is more fluid, and things can happen more spontaneously. Plans are made, but with the understanding that they may be changed, even at the last minute, depending on circumstances. Punctuality is not a virtue, and many things can take precedence over adherence to a schedule.

Chinese-American Interaction

The bulk of China's immense history is as an agrarian society, and even today over half of the Chinese work force remains involved in agriculture. For the farmer, life is not linear, but an infinite cycle of seasons, of sowing and reaping. In addition, Chinese put more value on the importance of maintaining relationships and harmony than they do on the swift completion of tasks. Where Americans say "Time is money," Chinese proverbs teach that "You can't buy an inch of time with an inch of gold." Add to that the behemoth of Chinese bureaucracy and the lack of urgency endemic to most government-run enterprises, and you might wonder how things ever get done in China.

The most common complaints in Chinese and American inter-actions revolve around time. Americans complain that they can't get prompt responses from the Chinese, who in turn feel pressured by the Americans, who don't understand that for various reasons, things very often just take more time.

Patience has long been a virtue in China. Americans often find that in negotiations their Chinese counterparts can take advantage of the Americans' short timeframe and their general impatience to conclude a deal, using time as a bargaining chip. The pace of American business means that the typical reaction to a lack of response from a negotiating partner is to bargain further, to lower the price or somehow sweeten the deal in order to get an immediate response. Chinese who know this can use it as a nego-tiating tactic, particularly when the Americans are under pressure to wrap things up within a matter of days. Additionally, it is important to understand that often the failure to respond or the lack of urgency on the part of the Chinese may be due to the exis-tence of a political system that makes people afraid of being held accountable. Therefore, each individual waits until the group reaches a consensus.

Time Tips

- Be prepared to be patient. You will not change the Chinese timetable by pressing them to hurry. In fact, doing so is likely to cause more harm than good.
- Most Chinese are well aware of the impatience of the typical American, and many use it to their advantage. Don't let your impatience get the best of you.
- Adjust your timetable and expectations to the Chinese culture. Pad the time you allot for a visit, delivery, or other business deal. If you are in a negotiation, be prepared to make follow-up trips. This will help negate any advantage the Chinese might hope to gain by playing a waiting game.

COMMUNICATION

When you say one thing, the clever person understands three things.

—Chinese proverb

Al Baker checked his e-mail again, for the hundredth time that day, it seemed. Nothing. Why wasn't the China office responding? Yesterday he had sent his fourth e-mail asking for the status of a financial report he was supposed to have received from them last week. He had sent this last e-mail to several different people, hoping that at least one of them would respond. He had tried every tactic he could think of to get the information, from asking nicely to something just short of a threat. Now it looked like he was going to have to have his boss, the vice president, contact the vice president in the China

office to see what was going on. None of this would be happening if the people over there would just do their jobs!

Direct versus Indirect Communication

What is the goal of communication? Regardless of what culture you are from, you need to be able to relay information to other people. But is that the goal in and of itself, or are there other variables that affect the goal?

In cultures that value direct communication, the goal of communication is mainly to relay information. Value is placed on being able to state your point in a clear and concise manner, and words have limited nuances. In general people do not appreciate having to pull the real point out from a surfeit of words.

If you are an indirect communicator, on the other hand, you have to take other factors into account. It may be important not to cause offense to your listener, to show deference, or to maintain harmony, for example. Very often the real meaning in indirect communication cultures is a subtext buried under many layers of meaning or intertwined with nonverbal clues or metaphor.

Chinese-American Interaction

One of the most important facets of the Chinese culture is the concept of "face." Most Westerners have some understanding of what this means, but it is limited by other characteristics of Western culture which define it. The desire to avoid embarrassment is universal; however, when and why one should be embarrassed is not.

Face, in its Eastern form, is a responsibility between two people that requires participation by both parties. There are many different aspects of face. Westerners are usually familiar with "losing face" and "saving face." But in the Western view, both of these ideas are seen in a more individualistic perspective; they all revolve around the self. One loses or saves one's own face; others are involved only in the role of the audience in front of whom this small drama occurs.

Chinese, on the other hand, have many more phrases to

describe their broader definition of the term. In addition to "losing face" and "saving face," Chinese speak of "protecting face," and "giving face." Thus face becomes an interactive exercise. An individual's motivation moves from the selfish protection of his or her own image to include the desire to enhance and protect the prestige of others as well.

The idea of face is closely tied to Confucian ideals. It is the natural conclusion of a system in which moral behavior stems from mutual concern and takes the form of reciprocal relationships.

Face has a direct impact on the way we communicate. In a society which values face, it becomes important that one not deliberately offend or insult the person with whom one is speaking. This would negatively impact the face of both parties. Therefore it becomes important to maintain harmony between people and avoid open conflict. This is best accomplished with an indirect approach to communication.

Westerners often fail to fully appreciate the importance of face in Asian societies. One's face is one's reputation. Preserving one's reputation and prestige is not just a loose social guideline, it is a moral obligation. Statements or actions that seem to an American to be harmless—or even helpful—can cause discomfort or even, in the worst case scenario, damage a relationship beyond repair. For example, an American subordinate who attends a meeting where his boss is presenting would think nothing of raising a question, of making an alternate suggestion, or even of disagreeing with the boss in front of other people. In China, this type of action causes damage to the face of both parties—to the boss for having been criticized in front of others and to the subordinate for shaming his boss in such a way.

Interactions between people in the United States lack the interdependence inherent to Chinese relationships. Without interdependence direct communication becomes possible and, in the case of the United States, desirable. Emphasis is placed on clear and concise communication rather than mutual protection of face.

The group is seen as a source of strength and comfort in China, and business decisions are generally made on a basis of consensus, within the framework dictated by the top person, be it a politician or the CEO of the firm. If you encounter silence or vague, elusive answers from a particular person you are dealing with, it is often because the final decision must be made by group consensus or through a process higher up and out of sight. The view of this person you are dealing with must be in line with that decision. This person will not tell you he is waiting for the group decision because he will "lose face" by admitting he is not the one who is making the decision.

You might say that a relationship is like a stream on whose banks two people stand opposite each other, and communication is the stones lying in the water between. Americans use the stones to build a bridge across the stream so that they can find common ground. Chinese, however, place the stones along the sides of the stream. As each person places stones along the banks of the stream, it is kept peacefully running its course. When a stone is carelessly placed, however, it can cause the stream to overrun its banks; when dropped into the stream, the stones will eventually create a dam, effectively halting the flow of the river. So when an American is in China, he might well find himself standing over the river with his half of the bridge built, wondering why his Chinese counterparts are busy shoring up the banks on the opposite side.

Communication Tips

- Remember that Chinese people have an indirect style of communication. Be careful not to speak too bluntly.
- Do not underestimate the importance of "face." Make it a point to keep face and to maintain the face of others.
- Most Chinese prefer not to say "no" outright. Learn to properly interpret the meaning behind phrases such as "perhaps" and even "yes."

GROUP DYNAMICS

No matter how big, one beam cannot support a house.

—Chinese proverb

Peter Chen was troubled by the atmosphere in his office. After six months in the United States, Chen still wasn't sure he understood his American staff. They did not seem to be able to work together as a team. Every member of the group appeared to have his or her own agenda; were they even working toward the same goal? In meetings they argued constantly, then they took votes to see who agreed with whom. Chen thought that they must all be dedicated to their jobs—after all, they all stayed well past 5:00 P.M. virtually every day—but he wondered how they ever got anything done, since they couldn't seem to agree on anything.

Group-oriented versus Individualistic

In the overall scheme of things, which is stronger: the needs of the individual or the needs of the group? Is it usually the case that individuals are willing to make sacrifices for the good of the group, or will the group suffer for the benefit of the individual?

We are all faced at one time or another with making a decision to place someone else's needs before our own—our family, our friends, our team at work. Where the deeper cultural differences lie, however, is in the expectations of society. What is the societal norm for looking out for oneself or one's group? The next time you stay late at the office, think about your motives for doing so. Are you really staying to finish the project because it will be an enormous benefit to your company? Or are you staying because in order to advance up the ladder of success it is important that you be perceived as dedicated and hard-working?

Groups can take on many forms. Your group might consist of your family (immediate or extended), co-workers, the company you work for, friends with whom you grew up and went to school, a tribe or clan, a religious group, or a local, regional, or national affiliation. And of course you may belong to many different groups throughout your life.

If you are group-oriented, the group is an inherent part of your identity. You are first and foremost Japanese or a Muslim or Bantu or a member of the Fuentes family, and a major factor in your decisions and actions is how they affect other members of your group. As an individual you are much more inclined to align your own goals with that of the group. Your talent is part of a larger pool, and when you cooperate with others in your group it becomes possible to reach a mutual goal.

For example, some of the sales people in your division brought in more revenue and some less. However, the important thing is that the sales goals were met, so everyone should share equally in the annual bonus. In this way, individual weaknesses are balanced by others' strengths so that a balance is achieved. The success of the team will strengthen it and encourage people to strive for higher goals.

The sales scenario wherein everyone shares equally in the bonus when some people have brought in more business than others seems unfair in individualistic cultures. Sure, it's great that we met our sales goal, but since I was responsible for more revenue than the other members of the team, I should receive a greater share of the annual bonus. If everyone got an equal share of the bonus, people would be tempted to coast along and not put maximum effort into their jobs. As a member of an individualistic culture, it is important that everyone receive the recognition due him or her and, conversely, that everyone take responsibility for his or her mistakes.

A culture's inclination toward the group or the individual will be an important influence in areas such as teamwork, rewards and motivation, and decision making.

Chinese-American Interaction

A group orientation, or collectivism, is inherent to the Confucian society. In order for the five relationships defined by Confucius—and therefore society—to function smoothly, it is necessary for individuals to subject their own desires to the greater good of the group. People do not exist independently of one another, and an individual is defined by his or her relationship to the group.

Group orientation remained firmly in place as China moved from an imperial system to communism, which also holds collectivism as an ideal. It is true that China today is moving toward more individualism, due to recent social and political changes, but the long history and deep roots of group coordination must not be underestimated.

Group orientation, of course, implies a reciprocal relationship in which the individual benefits from the group as well as vice versa. Until very recently in China, a big part of this relationship was the so-called Iron Rice Bowl, where every worker was guaranteed life employment and would never have to worry about going hungry. Beyond the Iron Rice Bowl, most companies, in fact, also provided housing for their employees.

However, more recently the Iron Rice Bowl has begun to rust. Private companies, and even the government, can no longer guarantee lifetime employment. Goals have shifted to include profitability as well as social welfare, leading to both greater opportunity for individuals and a smaller and somewhat torn social net.

The United States, on the other hand, is staunchly individualistic. Individual rights are guaranteed by law, and each individual is expected to reap the rewards (or consequences) of his or her own actions. Individual expression is encouraged from an early age. Americans are defined by what they have accomplished (usually in terms of career), rather than by group membership.

In spite of the newly entrepreneurial spirit in China, group orientation is alive and well in China in many ways, especially in comparison to the United States. It affects people's expectations of one another and how they interact; you will see it in how decisions are made and how negotiations are conducted, in reward systems, and how people work in teams.

Tips on Group Dynamics

- Work with the group, not against it. When meeting with Chinese, expect to give them time to process topics as a group without expecting an immediate response.
- Many people are reluctant to voice an individual opinion, especially in front of a superior. If you wish to incorporate individual initiatives, such as freely offering ideas in a brainstorming session, be sure you lay the groundwork first. Expect that it can take a considerable amount of time to implement such a plan.
- Realize that people's priorities and expectations may be different than yours because of group dynamics. Take time to observe and understand how the Chinese groups you encounter function, be they a negotiating team, coworkers, or employees.

STATUS & HIERARCHY

Experience is a comb which nature gives to men when they are bald.

—Chinese proverb

Joshua Pine was growing frustrated in his position as Regional Manager in the Beijing office. He knew he had a lot of very bright people on his staff, but they were resisting his attempts to empower them to take action on their own. He still had his assistant managers approaching him to approve every little thing, and even to make their decisions for them. He certainly wanted to support his people, and he made it a point to always be available to offer advice, but he couldn't do everyone's job for them—how would he ever get his own job done?

Ascribed versus Achieved Status

Social strata are inherent in all cultures. How we differ is in the way that we gain and attribute status. Do we acquire status by virtue of who we are or by what we do?

Status can be based on the inherent characteristics of a person, over which we have no control, such as age, race, gender, or family background. Or it may be based on what a person has accomplished, including educational and professional qualifications, such as the school one attended or whether one is a sign painter or a doctor.

Certainly when we evaluate other people we use a mixture of these two criteria. However, a culture will generally value one over the other. In an ascribed status culture, for example, an employee must show competence in order to advance in his or her job; however, he or she must also have seniority. The wisdom and experience that come with age are valued. Similarly, a manager might be influenced in his or her hiring decisions by the applicant's family background or social connections—or lack thereof. Social strata are generally well-defined and one does not easily move among them.

It is much more common in achieved status cultures to accord status based on accomplishments. Social strata are less defined and it is not uncommon to move up the social ladder. While there are certain benefits that come with seniority, it is certainly possible for younger employees to be promoted above their elders. A person's past and, perhaps more importantly, perceived future performance is valued above age. Many U.S. companies, in fact, have a certain number of "fast track" employees who are expected to move up quickly through the ranks based on their potential performance.

Vertical versus Lateral Hierarchy

Another aspect of status is whether the hierarchical structure is vertical or lateral. Hierarchy is something that exists in all cultures, whether hidden or overt. In a vertical hierarchy, the structure tends to be overt. Positions within the hierarchy, corporate or social, are clearly outlined, and it is expected that people show and receive the respect due to them as a result of their position within the hierarchy. This respect is shown in many ways, from the use of titles to the depth of one's bow to the vocabulary one uses. The expatriate manager who tries to get his subordinates to call him "Dave" in a vertical hierarchy probably isn't going to have much luck—his employees will feel uncomfortable using such a disrespectfully familiar form of address to their boss. The title "Mr. Dave" may be the closest his subordinates come to using his first name.

Lateral hierarchies allow more equality among colleagues. Each person must be respected for his or her ability, regardless of position in the company. The more egalitarian nature of lateral hierarchies usually means a more informal environment. Lateral hierarchies also allow for greater empowerment at lower levels, as most decisions related to their jobs are made by employees themselves; there is less direct instruction from superiors. There is less concern for following the exact lines of authority than there is for finding the person who is in a position to take care of the issue at hand. Therefore, an employee who needs information from someone in another part of the business would have the freedom to approach that person directly, rather than channeling the request up through his boss, then on to the other person's boss, and finally down to the person who has the information, a restriction that an employee in a hierarchical organization would find difficult to circumvent.

You will find that a culture's views of the nature and importance of status influences business in the relationship and interaction between superiors and subordinates, in the way that information flows (or does not flow) among individuals, in the decision making process, and in how people move up through the ranks, to name but a few.

Chinese-American Interaction

A hierarchical structure is inherent in the Confucian philosophy. The very basis of Confucian relationships is the obedience of those in lower levels to those in higher levels. This hierarchy is present today in China, both on the societal and organizational level.

It is interesting to note that business people, or those involved in commerce, traditionally occupied the lowest position in the societal totem pole. The notion of trading for profit was contrary to the Confucian principle that a moral person is concerned more for the well-being of his fellows than for his own benefit. Individual profit-seeking is a selfish motivation in a collective society. Of the four traditional social classes, intellectuals occupied the highest ranks, followed by peasants, workers, and finally businessmen. The path followed by intellectuals often led to official positions, the only suitable occupation for someone in that class. In recent years, however, business has gained credibility as a reputable occupation.

To understand the Confucian hierarchical structure, it is important to remember that the Chinese culture contains an element of egalitarianism. For Chinese, however, egalitarianism has a different meaning than for Americans. In the Western sense, egalitarianism means that each individual has equal standing and equal opportunity within the society. This means that a person can make of himself what he will; one is limited only by oneself. However, egalitarianism in China refers to equality within a social rank. Limitations are imposed by society in the form of a hierarchical structure; egalitarianism exists within that structure. For example, within one social rank there should be economic equality. While social stratification is accepted, the appropriate allocation of wealth within that framework will ensure that everyone remain content. This reasoning means that in state operated enterprises the salaries are low but everybody is earning the same thing. An equal outcome is the goal, rather than equal opportunity.

The Chinese and American ideals of hierarchy versus egalitarianism can come into conflict in many different ways. Our perceptions of hierarchy have an impact on the way we interact with people, the way we communicate, and the way we see "fairness" (or lack of it) in the world.

Tips on Status and Hierarchy

- Remember that you will need to respect the lines of hierarchy. For example, decisions can only be made at certain levels; pressuring someone who is not able to make a decision will not help.

• Respect is an important part of the Chinese culture. It is important to use people's titles and last names, not their first names.

RELATIONSHIPS

*Only when all contribute their firewood
can they build a strong fire.*

—Chinese proverb

Yang Yuching was participating in a trade mission to the United States. His goal was to find potential partners for his company, which was a small but growing clothing assembly plant. He had excellent contacts in China, which meant that he was able to produce very high-quality products at a very good price. If he could find a company in the United States that needed his products, together they could have a booming business. In addition to pursuing some of his own contacts, he had decided to come on this trip, since it was co-sponsored by the Chambers of Commerce of his city and its American sister city. By the end of his stay, however, Yang was doubtful that he would be able to find a business partner this way. He had met many Americans, and they were all very friendly, but none of them seemed very serious about doing business with China. At the receptions and meetings the Americans would flutter around like butterflies, hopping from one person to another. Several Americans had expressed interest in Yang's products, and had told Yang to get in touch with them, but were they really serious? How could they be, after ten minutes of conversation?

Relationship-oriented versus Task-oriented

In the business of life, what takes the priority: your personal relationships or the tasks you do? If you are from a relationship-oriented culture, relationships come before tasks, and, in fact, may be necessary in order to perform tasks. This can have many implications. A sickness in the family (even the extended family) may take precedence over work; a chance meeting with a friend might delay a scheduled meeting; a deal might not be struck until both parties have had time to build a basis of mutual respect and trust. Relationships—ones that go beyond just working together—are the cornerstones of a life of interdependent networks and are a goal in and of themselves.

Task-oriented folks, on the other hand, tend to focus on the job at hand and leave the relationships to whatever time is left over after the work is finished. No friendship or personal intimacy is necessary to perform your job and it is generally considered more professional not to let your personal life intrude on your work. The general

rule is that you should get on with your business and worry about "being friends" later.

This is not to say that relationship-builders don't get things done; nor is it meant to imply that task-focused people are not friendly. It simply means that the expectations you have in your personal and business relationships might not be the same as what is expected in another culture. If you are doing business abroad, you will find that these differences can be crucial to your success. You will see them crop up in negotiating, making deals, getting information, making sales, organizing joint ventures, and forming teams, to name but a few areas.

Chinese-American Interaction

An understanding of the Chinese concept of *guānxì* is vital to success in China. *Guānxì* means connections, but it is much more than a rolodex full of names. It is more like a spiderweb, woven as the means to accomplish a goal—dinner in the spider's case, but virtually every aspect of life in the case of the Chinese. The network of relationships is carefully cultivated, and it is what enables an individual to get things done.

Take the example of the infamous Chinese bureaucracy. If you are an exporter of goods, there is most likely a limit on the total quantity of any one item that can be shipped from the country, which means that you have to apply to the government for the right to export your goods. The better your connections, the better your chances of receiving an allocation to export. If you have no connections with the right people, either directly or indirectly, you will have to wade through the red tape as best you can, but your chances of ending up with a slice of the pie are slight.

Like face, relationships are a reciprocal obligation. One favor begets another until the web is intricately woven, binding people together. To the task-oriented American, these relationships can smack of favoritism in the best cases and bribery in the worst, a practice that is generally taboo to Americans. But to Chinese, this network is a time-honored system of interpersonal ties.

Traditionally, Chinese must know and trust one another before being able to conduct business, initially preferring to spend time developing a relationship before a contract is signed or an agreement is made. Americans, however, generally view business relationships as something that may (or may not) evolve, but are not necessary to begin, or even conclude, the business deal.

Viewed from a historical perspective, there is nothing strange about this. The Confucian society encourages interdependence, relying on those relationships and the trust that grows from them to ensure that obligations are met. The United States, however, rests on a legal foundation. Thus contractual obligations in the U.S. replace a relationship as the basis of trust.

Relationships in China Today

Modernization, privatization, and competition have weakened the system of guānxì. As the legal system stabilizes and competition increases, Chinese are developing a more task-oriented approach to business. Obligations to a relationship must be weighed against the bottom line.

For example, if you are in charge of procurement in a state owned factory and are in need of a fabric supplier, it makes sense for you to turn to your cousin, who owns a textile mill. In that way you fulfill a family obligation and also strengthen the guānxì between the two of you against a future reciprocal favor. The environment in state owned enterprise fosters the use of relationships because it is not generally profit driven.

If, however, the factory is privately owned, you are answerable for profitability. If your cousin's prices are higher than that of another supplier, you will lose profit as well as hinder your ability to compete, leading to lost business.

This does not in any way mean that guānxì has been eradicated. Guānxì continues to grease the wheels of business on many different levels. It facilitates your interaction with coworkers, with outside business contacts, and with the government. It continues to be an important part of the Chinese culture, merely tempered by the advent of a market economy.

Relationship Tips

- Despite some changes over the past few decades, relationships continue to be an important part of the Chinese culture. Don't underestimate their value.
- Take the time to build relationships with your Chinese colleagues and associates. You will be able to accomplish a great deal more if you first build a solid relationship.

REASONING

The beginning and the end reach out their hands to each other.

—Chinese proverb

As part of her goal to expand into the global marketplace, Alex Markham traveled to China to meet with a potential business partner. Alex, a small business owner, hoped to export her line of cosmetics to China and had found an interested Chinese distributor. She had carefully prepared her presentation for her Chinese associates, and was anxious to get started, since she had both a limited time frame and a limited budget. After spending quite some time on introductions and greetings, her Chinese host invited her to take the floor. She began by telling them what her sales projections were to be sure she had everyone's interest, then described her product, emphasizing the quality of the cosmetics. Finally, she mentioned the terms that she was proposing.

When she finished her presentation, she encouraged the Chinese representatives to ask any questions they had. Their questions were about her company, how long she had been in business, her background, and so on. Finally, the Chinese began their presentation. Like their questions, however, their presentations focused not on the product or the deal, but on the history of their company. Alex was bewildered.

She wondered if there was some sort of communication problem, or if the Chinese weren't interested in her cosmetics for some reason.

Pragmatic, Analytical, or Holistic Reasoning

Perhaps the most complex manifestation of culture is found in our thought processes. Around the world the way people reason can be divided into three general styles: pragmatic, analytical, or holistic.

Pragmatic thinkers begin with the goal and seek the steps that will enable them to attain that goal. The emphasis is therefore on finding practical ways to solve a problem or reach a goal. For example, if the goal is to increase sales by 10% in a given year, the task is then to identify the means of doing so. A pragmatic thinker will, for example, compile information on increasing his or her client base and the purchases made by current clients. The pragmatic thinker's final report might include a brief mention of all of the ideas which were presented, but its most prominent point will be the recom-

mendation of certain sales strategies and how best to implement these strategies.

Analytical thinkers take the reverse approach, focusing on the process with the goal as the logical conclusion. So an analytical thinker's approach to the problem above of increasing sales by 10% will be different. He or she will begin by exploring all options, including increasing client base and increasing purchases. From there the analytical thinker will select the strategies that will be the most beneficial, leading to the conclusion that it is possible to increase sales by 10% in a given year. This increase then becomes the goal.

Holistic thinkers incorporate both of the methods above, but they also tend to include elements in their thinking that most pragmatic and analytical thinkers would not. In determining sales, a holistic thinker would examine the information gathered on the potential and current client base, but he or she might also add a few things to the mix. For example, a holistic thinker may ask, what are the possibilities of expanding the current range of products? Even if the pragmatic and analytical thinkers above had thought of this scenario, it is much more likely to be in a linear fashion. That is, a seller of office products who is not a holistic thinker would not get into selling, say, women's lingerie. Holistic thinkers tend to be more nonlinear in their thinking and may see a relationship between office products and women's lingerie that pragmatic and analytical thinkers do not, such as the fact that they have a ready supplier of both. Another example of a potential question asked by a holistic thinker is what the impact would be on the sales staff. Will the higher quotas require them to work more hours in the week or spend more time away from their families? Finally, after putting all of the pieces in the puzzle, the holistic thinker will see that it is possible to increase sales by 10%.

As you can see, each of the three scenarios above ended up in the same place: a 10% increase in sales. However, the road taken in each instance traveled through different terrain, different countries, even. This difference in reasoning styles has an unmistakable impact on doing business abroad. Its significance is readily apparent in the process of decision-making, of writing reports and making presentations, and even in communicating.

Chinese-American Interaction

Americans are widely regarded as pragmatic reasoners, while the Chinese are holistic thinkers. Americans focus on the goal and on getting there. Once the goal is identified, the appropriate course of action can be chosen to achieve that goal. Industry and company data provide the information necessary to plot this course.

In a Chinese business, there may be external factors that influence the goal and the path to it. These can be any number of things, such as interpersonal relationships, obligations to the community or employees, and even, in some cases, superstition. For example, a Chinese businessperson may choose to order supplies from a relative or friend, even though the prices may be slightly higher. This may be done with the expectation of future reciprocal business or perhaps even a sense of familial duty. Such concerns have until recently been prioritized over simple profitability.

Fēng Shǔi

Another example of these differences might be the location of a site for a new plant. An American company will look at the cost to build and maintain, tax issues, and the availability of workers in the area. A Chinese company will take into account these considerations, but they may also consider the location on a more metaphysical plane.

Many Chinese practice *fēng shǔi*, a belief that every physical location is influenced by a positive or negative energy. *Fēng shǔi* managed to survive the Cultural Revolution and is still practiced today. It was reintroduced into China by overseas Chinese, especially people from Taiwan and Hong Kong doing business in China. It recently began to take hold in the West, as well.

Fēng shǔi arose from the traditional belief that China rests on the Earth Dragon, around whom wind (*fēng*) and water (*shǔi*) interact. It was the job of *fēng shǔi* experts to determine if the location in question—the site of a new building, a battlefield, etc.—was located in an auspicious or advantageous place. The back of the dragon was considered a prime location, the neck a bad location and the eye of the dragon the absolute worst location. An improper location or even a building facing in the wrong direction is thought to invite negative forces.

Fēng shǔi is about balance and harmony. It is based on the premise that there are five basic elements in the world bound together in the circle of life: fire, water, metal, wood, and earth. Each and every one is an important part of the world, and none are "bad." The key is to balance the elements to minimize the adversity in your surroundings and thus optimize your chances of health and prosperity.

Although there are some basic "dos & don'ts" in *fēng shǔi*, it is largely specific to the individual and is based on both the event of your birth (date, time, and location) and the where and how you live your life. For that reason, it is necessary to consult a *fēng shǔi* expert who can correctly interpret the flow of energy around you. If you are interested in delving further into the complexities of *fēng shǔi*, there are myriad books, Web sites, and other resources currently available. While government officials and academics may tolerate the practice, there are people who still think *fēng shǔi* is superstition. Therefore it may be wise not to bring it up when dealing with officials.

Tips on Reasoning

- Our need for information can differ based on our reasoning style. If you remember from the above paragraphs, the Chinese style is largely holistic, while the American style is mostly pragmatic. With that in mind you will be able to provide the full range of information that will satisfy your Chinese colleagues.
- Don't underestimate the roles that seemingly irrelevant issues, such as relationships, duty, or what you may regard as superstition, can play in decision making.

WHAT DOES IT ALL MEAN?

As you have probably already noticed, there are often correlations between the above categories. None of the six categories exists in a vacuum. If relationships are more important to you, it follows that you will be more willing to spend time (or waste it, from a task-oriented point of view) getting to know people before plunging into the task; relationship-oriented cultures tend to also be flexible time cultures. Similarly, if strong and harmonious relationships are your goal, that will be reflected in the way you communicate; relationship-oriented cultures also tend to be indirect communication cultures. You see the pattern.

China is a complex culture and one that, since it sits virtually opposite the United States in each of the six cultural categories, is often difficult for Americans to understand. While Americans value time, direct communication, pragmatic thinking, and so on, Chinese value relationships, a sense of structure, and a more encompassing viewpoint. Add to that the dimensions of change that recent years have brought and you have modern China. As a visitor to China, it behooves you to learn about the Chinese culture and, more importantly, to adapt your schedule, your communication style, and even your ways of doing business to ensure a mutually beneficial relationship with your Chinese business colleagues and friends.

THREE

LIVING ABROAD: Thoughts Before You Go

Most people face an international move with a combination of excitement and apprehension. Moving within the confines of your home country can be difficult enough; moving across borders adds a whole new dimension of cultural differences which can magnify the stress we all naturally feel in a new environment.

The single most important thing that you can do to ensure a successful sojourn abroad is to have realistic expectations. Unfortunately, it's difficult to gauge how realistic your expectations are before you go. You can, however, help define your perspective by considering the following points.

- **What do you hope to get out of your stay abroad?** If you will be working while you're abroad, your company will have certain expectations about the goals of your job, but it is up to you to set your own goals for personal and professional development. Be specific. Although "broadened horizons" is an admirable goal, "gaining an understanding of the domestic automotive market" is a marketable skill that you will be able to use. If you will not be employed, it is essential that you make plans now for how you will occupy your time in the new country. What skills and interests do you have that you can apply to your advantage? You will have many options, including volunteering, continuing your education, or developing a hobby or skill into a freelance business.

- **If you have a partner and/or children, are you starting out with a sound relationship with your partner and with your children?** Although it may be tempting to regard an international assignment as a time to make a fresh start, it is not advisable to use the assignment to try to mend a troubled relationship. An inherent problem with living abroad is the stress caused by living in a new environment and the additional stress of confronting a foreign language and culture. A marriage or partnership that is in trouble, or a family with strained relationships, is more likely to crumble with the added pressure. Couples and families who start out with healthy relationships often find that their ties are strengthened by an international assignment. Each person is able to offer the support and encouragement necessary to create a positive environment with open lines of communication.

- **How much do you know about daily life in the country you are moving to?** It's one thing to know about the history of a country, to be familiar with the cultural icons and know where the best hotels are. But how much do you know about the infrastructure of the country? How much does it cost to live there? What is it like to go shopping? What is the definition of "service" in that country? Will you be able to find babysitters, go to a nightclub alone, wear shorts, ski? In other words, will you be able to find all of the things that you count on to make your life easier and more pleasurable? And if you can't, can you live without them or find acceptable substitutes? These are very important questions to answer before you go. Most of the information is not difficult to find if you are willing to look for it. You can use the Internet, find books, or talk to people who have lived there.

Of course, you may not be planning this relocation alone, and, if not, there's a good deal to consider regarding your children and your partner. We'll start with the children.

IMPACT ON CHILDREN

Accepting an international assignment is a decision that affects everyone in your family, including children. Kids react in a variety of ways, including excitement, resentment and fear. Children can benefit enormously from living internationally. They develop the ability to look at the world multi-dimensionally, and the ability to interact successfully with a wide variety of people; they also tend to be open-minded and less judgmental. Unfortunately, at the beginning of an assignment, those benefits are on a distant horizon. What you have to deal with immediately is getting your children acclimated to their new lives as painlessly as possible.

Any kind of move can be difficult for children: being uprooted from friends and school and getting adjusted to a strange place is not easy. With an international move and the usual questions of "Will anyone like me?" and "Will I be able to make friends?", children have to deal with a new culture, where kids may look different, talk differently, or act differently—or all of the above. Fortunately, there are many steps you can take to smooth the transition.

First of all, involve children in the decision to move abroad. That is not to say that you must allow your child the chance to veto the move. The first reaction of most children to any move—domestic or international—is generally negative. (In fact, if a child reacts positively, it may be a sign of an underlying problem. Your child may be viewing the move as an escape hatch.) But you can let your child know as early as possible about the move. Take the time to discuss why the move is necessary. This is especially important for older children and teens. They are old enough to be involved in discussions about why this move will help Mom's or Dad's career.

Secondly, let your child express all of his or her feelings about the move. A child's emotions will probably run the gamut from anger to excitement at one time or another. Share your own feelings, too. Let your child know that it's a little scary for you, too, but also exciting. Most importantly, let your child know that it's okay to feel anxious, excited, scared or angry.

Another important way to help children adjust is to talk about expectations. Be optimistic, but prepare to accept the bad as well as the good. Don't hide the fact that it is going to be hard at times, but don't forget to emphasize the positive. Help your kids learn about their destination. Make it a family project in which you all participate. The more realistic your child's expectations are—and your own too, incidentally—the easier the transition will be.

An easy way to ease a transition abroad is to take items from the house and from your child's room that will make the new house or apartment feel like home. Continuity is a key factor in a child's adjustment. Even though it may be tempting to leave a lot of items and replace them when you get to your destination, try to take as many of your children's belongings as possible. It is worth the trouble of packing and shipping if your child's bicycle or her own familiar bed help her to become comfortable with her new home.

Just as you involved your children in the decision to move, involve children in the actual move as much as possible. Children feel helpless during an international move. They are being moved abroad without having much say in the matter. It will help lessen the feelings of helplessness if you let children make as many decisions as you can. Let your child choose favorite toys or furniture, a favorite picture from the living room or other items that you will take with you.

Allow your children the opportunity to say good-bye to their friends. Have a party and let the children invite their friends, or enlist the help of a teacher in throwing a class party. Take videos or lots of pictures to make an album to take with you. Adults are sometimes surprised that young children have as deep an attachment to their playmates and possessions as older children. With all children, it is important to recognize the sense of loss and grieving that children go through when moving. Making "good good-byes" is an important step in being ready to accept the new.

Finally, make plans for staying in touch with family and friends. Make an address book for younger children to write down the addresses of their friends so that they can write. Think about other ways to stay in touch, such as a round-robin newsletter, faxing, e-mailing or creating an audio- or videotape that you can send home. Create a schedule for a weekly or monthly telephone call, writing letters, or making your tapes.

There is no formula that you can use to determine how your child is going to react. And obviously two children in the same family can have totally opposite reactions, with one skipping cheerfully off to school right away and one suffering stomachaches which double him over in pain. Personality plays a part in the adjustment, but so do the parents and the environment created in the new home. Following are some descriptions of general behavior patterns. As you read these descriptions, consider how your child has reacted to stressful situations in the past; this will give you insight into how she might react to an international move—which is most assuredly stressful—and give some thought to how you can help her manage her cultural transition.

Infants and Toddlers

While the biggest disruption for infants is the change in sleeping and eating schedules, toddlers will have a harder time understanding what is happening, and will require a great deal of reassurance, before, during, and after the move. Distress at this age often results in a regression to babyish, clinging behavior.

Preschoolers

Preschool-aged children should be involved in the move as much as possible. Create ways that they can help, such as selecting which toys and clothing to bring and which to leave, labeling the boxes from their rooms, and packing for the trip. Seeing things being put into boxes and knowing that they will be unpacked in a few weeks is reassuring. Games will help explain the move; you can stage a play move with a dollhouse or by packing up and "moving" in your child's wagon. Coloring and activity books and picture books of your destination will add to the sense of security. Don't forget that shipped boxes may take several weeks to arrive. Make sure you take some of your familiar items on the plane with you.

Preteens

Older children will have more questions and will require more explanations. Take the time to discuss why you are moving, and be open about your feelings about moving. It helps children to know that their parents are sad to be leaving behind the people they know but are looking forward to a new experience. Learn with your children about your new country. Make trips to the library and select books that you can read together. Get a world map and a map of the country so they can see where they are going. Work with your children's teachers to make a presentation about the country. Learn about the food, traditional clothing, or holidays of the country. You can also help your children learn some phrases in the new language. Make a game of learning how to say "please" and "thank you" and other simple phrases. And give older children as much responsibility as possible in getting ready to move.

Teens

Teenagers often have the most difficulty with a major move. They are at a time in their lives when they are trying to establish an identity separate from their families and gain independence. The identity being shaped is linked to friends and social activities; changes make things all the more difficult. Moving to another country adds more pressure in the form of a potential language barrier and unknown customs. The best way to help teenagers through this period is with open communication. Let them know that what they are feeling is okay. You can also help by finding out as much information as possible about where you are going. Get information on the new school, including the curriculum and extracurricular activities. Finding out how kids dress and what they like to do when they get together is important too.

Although living abroad is a rewarding experience, some circumstances make it preferable to allow a teenager to remain behind for the remainder of a semester or a school year (especially in the case of high school seniors). Include your teenager in the discussion and make the decision based on the needs of your family.

All children, no matter what age, pick up on and, to a certain extent, reflect the behavior of their parents. Therefore, a positive attitude on your part is the best way to influence your children. Your enthusiasm and acceptance of your new life will help them adjust; the way you handle your own frustrations will set the example for them.

IMPACT ON SPOUSES OR PARTNERS

In the majority of cases, expatriates who accompany their spouse or partner abroad are not able to get the necessary permit to work in the host country. If you are giving up or postponing a career or job to make this move with your partner, you are suddenly faced with a great deal of free time that you will have to occupy in the new country.

Giving Up or Postponing a Career

At first glance, having several months—or even several years—of free time may sound like a dream come true. In fact, there are probably few people who wouldn't welcome an extended vacation.

However, you will find that after a couple of weeks of inactivity, you will begin to feel restless. For most people, a career provides a lot of their self-identity and feeling of self-worth, and its absence will certainly leave a void.

Being a Stay-At-Home Parent

When there are children in the family, the accompanying partner often decides to give up his or her career with the expectation that staying at home with the kids will provide more than enough to do. Before making this decision, here are a couple of issues to consider.

* How old are your children?
* Will your children be attending school?
* If your children will be in school, how do you plan to occupy your time when they are gone?
* Are there ways to get involved with your children's activities (i.e., volunteering at the school, coaching, leading field trips, etc.)?

DUELING CAREERS

The most pressing concern for dual-career couples is usually finding a position for the accompanying partner. It is important to stress that, while it is not always possible to find a paid position, there are usually plenty of other opportunities. The best way to find a "job" while you are living abroad is to redefine what "work" is. Broaden your definition from a nine-to-five job to include a host of other things, such as volunteering (which may lead to a paid position), freelancing, consulting, continuing your education, or learning new skills.

The following questions will help you begin to plan for identifying an occupation while you are abroad.

* Is it possible to get the permit you need to be eligible to work in that country? Can your company or your partner's company help you obtain one?

- Are there any opportunities within your company in the new location (either in a local office, if there is one, or as a consultant or working on a project for your company that can be accomplished from abroad)?
- Are there any similar opportunities within your partner's company?
- Are there entrepreneurial possibilities that you can pursue while abroad?
- Does either your company or your partner's company offer any type of career counseling or job location assistance that would help you find a suitable position abroad? (This can sometimes be negotiated as part of the relocation package.)
- Are there volunteer opportunities in your field that you would consider appropriate substitutes for a paid position?
- Are there other opportunities outside of your field that you would consider appropriate substitutes for a paid position?
- Do you have a hobby or other interest that you could capitalize on? For example, if you have an interest in photography, can you freelance or assist a professional photographer?
- Is this an opportunity to make a career change? You will have a period of time that you can put to use learning new skills or developing your skills in a different direction.

So far in this section we've taken a look at some important points to remember when considering the impact of a move abroad on yourself, your children, and your partner. Another major issue is cultural adaptation, or, in other words, what you should expect as you look ahead at your and your family's acclimation to a new culture.

UNDERSTANDING CULTURAL ADAPTATION

Culture shock, or cultural disorientation, is the result of finding yourself in a culture that is new and unfamiliar. People in the new culture not only speak a different language, they also live by a different set of rules, with different values, attitudes and behaviors. In some cases, these differences are immediately obvious; in others they are quite subtle. Cultural disorientation results in a range of emotional reaction, from irritation and frustration to anxiety and insecurity to resentment and anger. If the cultural adaptation process is not well managed, it will lead to depression.

No one is immune to culture shock; even frequent travelers and people who have lived abroad before feel its effect. The exception to the rule is the person who experiences mild culture shock in an abbreviated form. For the vast majority of sojourners, culture shock has a significant impact. The key to managing the cultural adaptation process is understanding what it is and developing an awareness of how it is affecting you personally. Once you reach this understanding, you will be ready to take steps to manage the stress caused by culture shock.

Culture shock is an emotional cycle with four distinct periods: enchantment, disenchantment, retreat, and adjustment. Although most people experience all four periods, each person's cycle is different; even different members of the same family will go through the ups and downs at different times.

Enchantment

Your arrival in your new home is an exciting time. Your senses are operating at top speed as you try to assimilate all of the new sights, sounds, and smells. You want to see and do everything. There are many new things to learn and discoveries to make. The differences that you notice between your home country and your new country are charming.

Disenchantment

After several weeks, a period of disenchantment typically sets in. As you establish your routine in your new country, reality begins to intrude on your enchantment. You have to deal with the mail carrier, the plumber, and your neighbors. Even simple tasks become difficult. When you go shopping, you may not recognize the food, and you may not be able to find what you want and what you're used to. People may seem rude, overly friendly, or just plain different. It is emotionally taxing to speak a new language, to use a new currency, and to perform all of the other minor details that you never gave a second thought to at home. With the new reality comes a sense of frustration and irritation, and often insecurity, since all of the cues you never had to think about before have changed.

Retreat

As you begin to feel more and more frustrated, tension and resentment will begin to build up. The retreat stage of the adjustment cycle is the most difficult. It becomes harder to leave your home. If you work, you may find yourself working late or coming straight home from the office. You turn down invitations and minimize contact with the culture and people in the new country. What was once "charming" or "interesting" about the country and customs has become "strange" and "stupid." In the constant comparison between your home country and the host country, home wins hands down. Homesickness is acute.

Adjustment

Finally, you will have to make the effort to adjust, to reestablish contact with the world and go on with your life. Your attitude will determine how you reconcile yourself to the things that are different in your new country. The people who make the most successful adjustments are those who realize that there are things that you like and dislike in any culture; doubtless there are things that you didn't care for at home, too. If you are willing to accept the culture, enjoy the things that you love about the culture, and find ways to accommodate the parts that you do not like, you will be happy. Once you have managed a successful adaptation, you will realize that you have gained a new set of skills, and are able to operate effectively within a new culture.

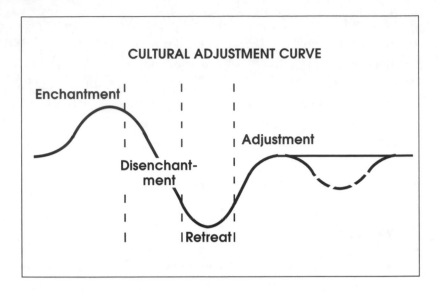

And Beyond

If you take another look at the Cultural Adjustment Curve, you will notice a second dip. Many people experience a second low period, or even a series of ups and downs. Just when you think you've finally got things figured out, you stumble again. Subsequent period of disillusionment might be more or less severe than the first; either reaction is normal.

KEYS TO A SUCCESSFUL ADJUSTMENT

The keys to a successful adjustment are self-awareness and acceptance. In order to be able to recognize cultural differences and effectively deal with them, you must first be aware of your own cultural values and attitudes.

Acceptance, the second key, means understanding that the culture, customs and rules in your new country, however far from your home country, are valid. Once you are able to accept them as different, rather than better or worse than your own, you will be more comfortable and able to adapt to new ways of doing things.

Understand that the ups and downs of cultural adjustment are normal; everyone who has moved before you has experienced the same process, complete with similar symptoms. If you reach out to those people, they can help you through the process. They will tell you that they survived and so will you.

Even after you have adjusted, you will have good days, when you feel at ease in your new culture, and bad days, when you question your sanity in deciding to move there. Once you have completely adjusted, the good days will eclipse the bad.

Coping Techniques

The psychological disorientation of an international move causes a tremendous amount of stress. In order to manage your cultural adaptation successfully, you must find an outlet for this stress. Think for a moment about how you relieve stress in your life right now. Stress outlets can be physical, such as jogging or biking, or mental, such as meditation or reading. List your stress relievers on a piece of paper. Once you've made your list, think about how you can continue those activities in your new home. Some of them— meditation, for instance—are easily transported. Some, however, may require modification or planning. For example, if you're used to riding your bike through the country lanes near your home but you will be moving to a crowded urban center, you may have to modify your activity. Can you use a stationary bike instead? Are there nearby parks or other areas where you can safely bike?

If you are not sure about the availability of a specific activity, make it a priority to find out. There are many resources, including other expats, people from your new country who may live in your area, consulates, books, and more.

FAMILIES

Families who have relocated to another country move with their own built-in support network to help each member through the process of adaptation. However, relocation also often means that family roles shift. A spouse who was a breadwinner before moving abroad might become a dependent; normally independent children may find themselves dependent on their parents, at least initially.

An international assignment often includes regional responsibilities that require frequent travel or extended business trips. If one partner is required to travel often, the other is left taking on more of the shared responsibilities in order to fill the gap left by the numerous absences. At times one feels like a single parent, even if it's not the case! Of course, the partner who is frequently away can find himself or herself feeling left out of the family upon returning.

All of these changes can be successfully managed if you have open lines of communication. Parents will benefit from talking with each other about the changes that are necessary to accommodate the new situation and by discussing ways that they can support each other to maintain consistency. The whole family will function better if everyone feels comfortable expressing fears and concerns and receives encouragement and support from other family members.

THE NONWORKING PARTNER

Unlike children and the working partner, a nonworking partner faces a new life that is without the inherent structure of school or work. So once the initial settling in is done, your partner goes to work every day, and the children traipse off to school, and you are left with nothing to do. If you were used to working, this is especially difficult. Even if you were not employed prior to the move, you still have left behind all of the familiar routines that filled your day.

According to article after article, many unsuccessful assignments are attributed to a nonworking partner who is unhappy in the new culture. This puts a lot of pressure on you; but with some effort and planning, you can put that particular worry aside.

In the absence of outside activities, the world of a nonworking partner is limited to household chores and the lives of children and the spouse. In the initial months, these same children and spouses have spent the majority of the day coping with their own stresses in the new culture and are rarely in the mood for scintillating conversation when they return to the sanctuary of home.

The more activities that you are involved in, the more fulfilled your own life will be. These activities can include your family, such as volunteering at your child's school, or they can be a pursuit of your own interests. The possibilities are practically endless. Other than volunteering, you can use the spare time to take classes, develop new skills, or pursue a hobby. If you give your imagination free rein, there are plenty of things that you can do. See the dual career sections throughout the book for other ideas on making the most of your time abroad.

CHILDREN

Children go through their own adjustment process, just as adults do. Younger children often feel frightened in a new location where everything is different from what they are used to: the people may look different, buildings may look different, and things certainly sound and smell different. Sometimes children (and adults, too) become an object of curiosity if they are living in a country where they look greatly different from the locals (for example, a blond child in Japan). They are often uncomfortable being stared at, touched, and patted by curious strangers. Younger children will have difficulty understanding what the move means and may tend to relate the move to vacations that they have experienced. They may be waiting for the trip to be over and for the family to return to their familiar surroundings at home. When the return home does not happen, they can get very upset. This may not happen for several weeks, or even months, so that a child who seems to have adjusted just fine may have problems down the road. Symptoms of their distress may be quite physical, such as stomachaches, or emotional, such as withdrawal and depression.

Older children, who do understand the implication of an international move and who realize that this move is not permanent, may be reluctant to get too deeply involved with friends, trying to protect themselves from the pain of making friends only to leave again after a year or two.

Throughout the process of adjustment, children will experience periods of anger. This is understandable since they have been dragged across the world against their wishes. It is important to allow children, whatever their age, to express their anger and to provide them with appropriate outlets for it.

Keep in mind, too, that younger children may not be able to put their feelings into words. You can help them express their feelings by taking along children's books about moving that will help them find the words to tell you what is wrong.

Naturally, all children will react differently to an international move. The best way to cope is with patience and understanding.

Global Nomads and Third Culture Kids

Global nomads, also called Third Culture Kids, are people who have lived overseas before adulthood, usually because of a parent's job. The global nomad is abroad without choice; the parents have chosen an international lifestyle, usually with the expectation that they will eventually return to the passport country. When children live abroad for a long period of time—or even for fairly short periods of time—they become culturally different from the parents. Their whole avenue of cultural exploration is very different from that of one born and reared in one place (as the parents often are).

Living internationally is a unique opportunity for children. It is a heritage that will shape the rest of their lives. While overseas, children develop a whole host of global skills, including multilingual skills, the ability to view situations from two different sides, and mediating and cross-cultural skills—simply by living. It is a heritage that can be applied very usefully in today's global arena.

One of the biggest challenges of moving abroad is to maintain the cultural identity of children. Children are absorbing the new culture through school, care givers and what they observe in the world around them. "Home" becomes a place to go on vacation once or twice a year. Parents can keep children connected to their own culture in a variety of ways, such as observing the holidays and traditions of their home culture. It is also helpful to keep in contact with what's going on at home, both with friends and family members and through magazines and newspapers.

PARENTING ABROAD

Raising a child abroad is an added challenge. Depending on where you are living, the values may be different than those you want to instill in your children. Children learn not only from their parents, but from school, peers, other caregivers, and society in general. Imagine that you have told your teenagers that they must be a certain age before they can drink, but they are suddenly confronted with vending machines in Japan which sell whiskey with no restrictions. This doesn't mean that Japan has a rampant problem with teenage alcoholism; it simply indicates that Japanese children are governed by different societal and parental restraints than your child. These kinds of problems are best dealt with by establishing very clear family rules. Have family meetings to establish and reinforce the rules.

A lack of organized activities for teenagers is often a problem. You and your child may have to actively search for the activities he or she likes to do. If you can't find appropriate activities, think about organizing a baseball team, a drama group, or other activities yourself. Encourage your children to bring their friends over, and try to meet their friends' parents, just as you would at home.

In some countries, the expatriate life itself can pose hazards in the form of making children accustomed to a higher standard of living than most people. Some people find themselves in a position to obtain household help. If you have never had this experience, it will take some time to be comfortable having someone work for you. You may have to train the people you hire, and you should definitely be clear on your expectations; do not assume, for example, that your idea of disciplining your children is shared by the person you hire to babysit your child.

If you are lucky enough to have household help, you may find that your children come to expect that someone will pick up after them and believe that they are not personally responsible for any chores. You may want to continue to assign some household tasks to children to reinforce your own values to them.

DUAL CAREER COUPLES

Dual career couples with children face the same issues as other families, but with an additional concern: child care. You are leaving behind your own child care network and will have to rebuild it from scratch. This can be complicated in countries where the extended family plays a major role in child care and public or private care is rare. Even if your children are in school, there may not be structured activities for them to participate in during the time between school and the end of the workday. There are options if you search for them. Think about the following ideas:

- Hire an au pair, nanny, or other live-in help.
- Look for formal or informal networks within the expat community; often there is a system of sharing child care.
- If your job has the flexibility, work from home or part-time.
- Approach a neighbor or another family about looking after your child during the day.
- Find an older person who would be interested in caring for your child (this has the added benefit of providing your child with a "grandparent").

If you are not able to find viable child care options, you may be able to create something that will meet your needs. And there are sure to be other families who would welcome the alternative. Don't rule out starting a day care center for younger children or organizing after-school activities for older children.

The most important thing, of course, is that you feel comfortable with your child care arrangements and that you trust the person who will be caring for your children.

THE SINGLE LIFE

Living abroad as a single person has both ups and downs. Moving to a place where you have no network of friends is difficult; coping with a new country and culture where you may not know how to go about meeting people to create your new social network is even tougher. In many countries, a person's work and home lives are kept quite separate. Social bonds have been formed throughout the years in school and elsewhere; business relationships do not necessarily translate into social relationships. And, in many cases, the family and extended family play a significant role in a person's life, and a great deal of time is spent in family activities. All of this can make it seem impossible for a newly arrived person to meet people and form friendships.

On the other hand, expatriates are often not subject to the same 'rules' as everyone else. Most expatriates find people in their host country to be very sympathetic to their situation, interested in learning more about them, and open to the possibilities of a relationship that extends beyond office hours. With luck, you will find yourself the recipient of invitations from your colleagues.

In the final analysis, though, it is up to you to build your new life. There are many avenues open to you. The best way to meet people, in fact, is to simply do something that you like to do. If you like to hike, go hiking; if you like to work out, join a gym. By doing something that interests you, you are putting yourself into situations where you can meet people with the same interests.

Another possibility to explore is the expatriate community. Where there are significant numbers of expatriates, there are usually networks in place, both for business and social purposes. Often there is a newcomer's club that provides activities and events for socializing. In these organizations, too, you will find people who have gone through the relocation and adaptation process and who have firsthand knowledge of what you are experiencing. These can be invaluable contacts throughout your own process of adaptation, giving you the support and encouragement you need, or even a shoulder to cry on when necessary.

Singles often have a unique experience abroad. Because they are not accompanied by a family, they generally have much more contact with the language and culture of the host country. An expat with a family goes home at the end of the day, speaks his or her native tongue at home, and is shielded from the language and culture to some extent. A single person does not have that shield, and spends more time speaking the new language and immersed in the culture through his or her social life. That person often has the added benefit of learning the language more quickly and thoroughly and of adapting to the new culture quickly.

THE GENDER FACTOR

The myth that women are not able to be successful in some cultures has largely been debunked. Instead, many experts say that, in fact, women are often better equipped to be successful than men. Most women find that they are viewed first and foremost as foreigners and are therefore not subject to all of the rules that apply to the local women. So even in cultures where women are not traditionally found in business, the same barriers do not apply to foreign women. In fact, many women have found that they can use the curiosity of local businessmen to their advantage and get their foot in the door more easily than their male counterparts.

One issue that women do face, on a very personal level, is whether or not they can accept the local culture—specifically the role and treatment of women. This does not mean that you have to behave exactly like the local women (although there may be a certain amount of conformity required of you), but you do have to be able to live with what is happening around you. This is a very personal decision; if you are uncomfortable with a culture's general attitude toward women, then perhaps it is better to wait for another assignment in a country where you feel more comfortable. Take care, though, that you understand the values that underlie the explicit behavior; it is easy to confuse the desire to protect with the desire to restrict.

THE RACE FACTOR

Most people of color find that they are seen first as being American, or Canadian, or British, etc. In countries where there is a history of discrimination against a certain minority group, usually an immigrant group, those rules simply do not apply to expatriates. There is no general formula for the experience that people of color have internationally. As in the case of one African-American, some expatriates feel that they actually have an advantage because they are used to being in the minority, which can make the adjustment to the new culture easier than for someone who is used to being part of the majority. As with the gender issue, it is not a question of the situation being good or bad; the issue is how you personally handle being in the limelight. In another case, a woman of Puerto Rican descent who grew up in New York considered herself to be an American and not a minority, with little thought of her cultural roots. When she was given an assignment in Latin America, she began to explore the Latino culture and began to value that part of her heritage.

There are cases, however, where Americans of a particular minority group do encounter difficulty abroad. This occurs most often when a person relocates to his or her ancestral home. For example, a Japanese-American might be selected for an international assignment in Japan. Usually the selection is made because of the "Japanese" part of the equation, with little thought to the "American" part. In other words, the selection is made because someone looks the part. This strategy can backfire, though. Even if that person speaks Japanese, he has absorbed the American culture and holds many American values since that is where he spent his formative years. The difficulty arises because he looks Japanese, but does not act Japanese. The result can be suspicion, distrust, or ostracism on the part of the Japanese. Similar situations confront many Asian-Americans whose families immigrated generations ago, including overseas Chinese, and Vietnamese-Americans. These issues can be minimized or avoided if you have an awareness of who you are and an understanding of the culture that you will be living in, especially the ways in which it is different from your own blended culture.

SEXUAL ORIENTATION

If you are lesbian or gay, you will probably want to do some research on the acceptance of homosexuals in the country you will be living in before you embark on your international assignment. While some countries have laws preventing discrimination against anyone because of sexual orientation, the acceptance of homosexuals by the society in general ranges from tolerance to homophobia much as it does in the United States. Make sure you are also aware of any laws prohibiting homosexual acts, and the possible consequences of practicing your sexuality. These concerns will affect bisexuals and transgendered people as well.

Moving abroad with a same-sex partner presents certain challenges not faced by married partners, as it is virtually impossible for an accompanying partner to get a work visa without being legally married. In addition, few companies include same-sex partners in the expatriate benefit package, causing complications in matters such as housing allowances, insurance and allowances for the loss of the partner's income. As an accompanying partner, you must focus on the alternatives that are available to you in the new country. Issues of giving up or postponing a career must be dealt with, and work alternatives must be investigated. Be proactive in exploring your options. Try to talk to people who have experience living in the country, both natives of the country and expatriates who have lived there. The more people you can talk to, the more complete a picture you will have about the implications of being lesbian or gay in your new culture.

A WORD ABOUT "EXPATRIATE CLUBS"

Many expats are wary of expatriate clubs, seeing them as a group of spouses who get together to play tennis and bridge. Even if there are people in the organization who do play bridge, the clubs are much more than that. Expat organizations are an excellent source of information on everyday issues, such as for finding a doctor; for networking, which accompanying partners who are seeking jobs or alternatives can tap into; for learning about the culture through structured activities and events; and for socializing. Each individual can decide how much he or she wants to be involved in the expatriate community. Indeed, there are plenty of expats who immerse themselves in it, and have very little contact with local-country nationals. There are also people who avoid it altogether. You are free to choose either, or any point in the spectrum between. Just keep in mind that the expatriate network can be invaluable; it can also provide that touch of home when you need it.

STAYING IN TOUCH

Even if you are excited about the prospect of living abroad, don't forget to make plans to stay in touch. You will want to hear from your family and friends at home, and keep them up-to-date on your own adventures. It's very easy to get swept up in your new life, and difficult to find the time to write or call with all of the new challenges of living abroad. However, the people who form your network of support will continue to be important as you adjust to your life abroad, especially during difficult times.

Establishing and maintaining a systematic way of communicating with home is also critical when it comes time to return after your sojourn abroad—something that is difficult to think about when you haven't even left yet!

It would be a good idea to pass your address in China on to your friends and relatives a month before you leave for China. Mail can take two weeks or more to get through and regular correspondence, especially in the first month after your arrival, provides an outlet for emotions and may well prevent you from feeling isolated. If it is possible, make some adhesive labels of your address in Chinese for your friends and relatives to use on envelopes to speed up delivery in China.

ROUND TRIP TICKET: THE RETURN HOME

Contrary to what you might think, the return home, or repatriation, after an international assignment is often a more difficult transition than moving abroad.

Professional Repatriation

One of the hazards of living and working internationally is that when you return, you can find yourself out of touch with your home office and with changes in your field or profession. Without proper preparation, you may find yourself without an office, without direction, and, indeed, without a job. Many former expats have returned to the home country after a successful assignment, only to have to wait for a suitable position to open up. In addition, many returned expatriates find that their experience abroad, and newly acquired skills and knowledge, are not put to use by the organization. A marketing manager fresh from an assignment in Latin America may find herself in a domestic marketing position, with little or no involvement in any Latin American markets. Even if the goal of the assignment was your professional development with an eye toward "globalization" or developing the international market, it is difficult to put those lofty goals to work practically. It is up to you to ensure that you are receiving the support you need during the assignment and to plan your strategy for reintegration into the home or local office.

If you moved abroad with your partner but were unable to work abroad, you face some of the same challenges when you return. You may feel that technology has passed you by, or that the skills you used before you moved are rusty from disuse. The best way to counteract this is to think about coming home while you are abroad and make sure that you keep your skills up to date—and maybe even develop new skills or expertise!

Following these steps can ease your professional reentry:

- Set a strategy before you go. Getting the support of upper management is crucial. Make sure you have a clear understanding of the objective of sending you abroad, what your goals are during the assignment, and exactly how you will fit back into the organization when you return.
- Stay in touch while you are abroad. In the case of international assignees, "out of sight, out of mind" holds true more often than not. Remind the home office of all of the points outlined above. Keep them informed about what you are doing and your accomplishments. And keep yourself informed about what is going on at the home office, promotions and staff changes, important policy changes, etc. E-mail and faxes are readily available in most companies; take advantage of technology to maintain contact.
- Find a mentor. In fact, find two or three. Mentors will help keep you in the minds of the decision and policy makers and keep you informed about what's going on at home. Mentoring relationships do not have to be formalized. And by finding several mentors, you won't find yourself returning from your assignment only to find that your champion in the company no longer works there!
- Visit the home office whenever you can. While you are on a home leave or business trip back, take the opportunity to reconnect with colleagues. Make use of the time to familiarize yourself with recent changes. Even if you take all of the recommended steps to stay in touch, understand that things will be different when you return. The fact is, the company and your colleagues have grown in the time you have been away, just as you have. It will take time and patience to reintegrate yourself into the new environment.

Personal Repatriation

Personal repatriation can also be painful. During your sojourn, you will have gained new insights and new perspectives. You will realize that there is really no right or wrong way to doing things, only different ways. In addition, most people remember "home" with fondness while they are away, forgetting about the things that aren't so great. And, of course, you will come home to find that your home country has its share of blemishes, just like everywhere else. This means that you will go through another cycle of adjustment as you refamiliarize yourself with your home culture and come to terms with the bad as well as the good in it.

If you are gone for several years, you will experience some disorientation when you return. Things will have changed, and you will have had a long period of time that you have not shared experiences with your family and friends. You may find that some people aren't interested in hearing about your experiences abroad, or who roll their eyes when you say "When I was in…" You may even encounter people who feel that you are putting on airs or that you feel superior because of your experience. You will have to come to terms with the fact that the people you knew before you left have changed, as you have, but in different ways.

There are ways to ease your personal readjustment.

- Stay in touch while you are gone. This can be difficult as you immerse yourself in your new life. Just as you fade from prominence at home, home fades for you. You will have to make a conscious effort to maintain regular contact, and make sure your kids do. The benefit of doing this is that when you return, there is less of a void in your experiences; you have kept people informed of important events in your lives, and vice versa.
- Visit home whenever possible. This is especially important if you have children. As well as helping you keep in contact with friends and family, it helps children maintain their sense of "home" and their cultural identity.
- Realize that your return home will have its ups and downs, just as your adjustment to living abroad did.

Children's Repatriation

The most difficult part of readjustment for children is that they have a gap in their lives where they have missed all of the pieces of popular culture that their friends have experienced, such as music, movies, TV, toys, and the way kids dress. They have to learn the current slang, and how kids talk. Along with this, they are different from their peers. They have developed in ways that kids at home have not, and they have a different frame of reference. More than adults, children who return home after living abroad will find that their peers see them as if thinking that they are superior and resent references to "When I was in..."

Tips for Staying in Touch

Most of us are accustomed to picking up the telephone and calling someone whenever we want. If you are living in another country, though, you may find that this isn't as easy any more because of time difference, poor phone service, or the prohibitive cost of international calls. Here are some suggestions for alternative ways of staying in touch.

- **The old standby: write letters.** Since the advent of the telephone, most of us are no longer letter-writers. When phoning is too expensive, this is one of the cheapest alternatives. However, it's also the slowest!
- **Fax letters.** Write your letter, then fax it. This will give you the satisfaction of instantaneous communication, without the prohibitive cost of an extended telephone call. Family and friends without a fax machine can probably arrange to receive faxes at a nearby copy shop or similar service center.
- **E-mail.** Probably the least expensive alternative, although not an alternative in all locations.
- **Chatting online.** If you and your family/friends all have Internet access, and you are able to access the Internet from your new country, try scheduling a time to find a quiet on-line corner to chat. Some of the larger services such as CompuServe and AOL offer service in many countries. Just remember that you may have to pay for local connect time rates—check with your service provider.

- **Use the company's phone.** With the company's permission, of course! As part of the expatriate package, some companies will allow you and your family members limited use of office phones to make international calls.
- **Videotapes or cassettes.** Although it will take a while to get there, videotapes and cassettes are more personal than writing letters. It's especially nice if you have children. You can exchange tapes with family members, and your children can exchange them with friends and even their classes at school. Be sure you will have access to the right equipment, since many countries use PAL instead of VHS. A further word of caution: be careful not to run afoul of the local laws. For example, in some countries, a videotape that includes your sister frolicking on the beach in a bikini may be considered pornography locally, even if you don't think it is. Make sure you know all of the applicable laws.
- **Write a newsletter.** This is especially helpful if you've got a long list of people you want to keep in contact with. Document what is happening in your life, write about the funny things that happen, about current events in your new community or anything else that appeals. Or start a round-robin letter, where everyone who receives the letter adds to the letter and passes it on to the next person.
- **Schedule regular phone calls.** It's bad enough to reach an answering machine when you want to talk to someone. It's worse when you are paying international rates to talk to a machine! If you talk to someone often, try to arrange for a regular time to call—every Sunday night at 10:00, the last Saturday of each month, or whatever fits both of your schedules.

LEARNING ABOUT YOUR NEW HOME

You're on your way to a new adventure. Now is the time to gather all of the information you need to make your international sojourn successful. Learning the language (if it's different from yours) and learning about the culture of your new home should be prioritized.

Learning the language of the country you will be living in is an obvious necessity. If it happens to be a language you already speak, great; if not, get started as soon as possible. Make it your goal to learn at least basic phrases before you go, more if possible. This book comes complete with a special language section and an audio CD for just that. While some people have a facility for learning languages, others find it more difficult. And it is often more difficult for adults than for children. Yes, you will make mistakes, and even embarrass yourself. It will be frustrating to have to struggle to express yourself, and you will feel awkward speaking with a limited vocabulary as you start out, but the effort is well worth it. The fact that you are willing to make the effort to adjust yourself to a new language will open many doors for you, and you will find that most people respond with delight. Learning the language also gives you the opportunity to really experience life in the local community in ways that are not possible if you are isolated from interaction by not speaking the local language.

Just as important as learning the language of your new country is learning about its culture and peoples. What are the values that the people hold, what is their history, what are their beliefs, customs and traditions? In the Background section of this book, we've provided you with enough of this kind of information to whet your appetite. Don't stop there, though! There are lots of ways to go about learning about the culture of your new country, including reading books and articles, talking to other expats or people from the country, and participating in a pre-departure (or post-arrival!) cultural orientation. Don't expect to learn everything there is to learn about the country in such a short time, or imagine that you will be prepared for every contingency; your goal is to learn enough to be comfortable in your new home. Once you arrive, you will discover on your own much more than you can ever learn from a book or from talking to other people.

Perhaps the first step in learning about your new culture is to learn about yourself and your own culture. Because culture is such an innate part of who we are, few people take the time to ponder what it is that makes them tick. Spend some time reflecting on your own cultural heritage, and ask yourself the same questions you would ask of another culture: What are your values, what is your history, what are your beliefs, customs and traditions? The more you understand about yourself, the easier it will be for you to recognize cultural differences and reduce the likelihood of cultural misunderstandings.

MOVING ABROAD "DOS AND DON'TS"

DO...

...*have realistic expectations.*

...*find out as much as you can before you go.*

...*learn the language—or at least basic phrases.*

...*be open-minded.*

...*find several mentors and cultural guides.*

...*make plans now for keeping in touch.*

...*take the initiative and reach out.*

DON'T...

...*lose touch with family and friends.*

...*wait until it is time to return to plan for your repatriation.*

...*wait for other people to come to you.*

FOUR

GETTING AROUND IN CHINA

ARRIVING IN CHINA

China, like other countries, has a specific procedure for foreigners entering the country. You will have been given an entry registration card, a health card, and a customs declaration form to fill out before you arrive.

The first part of the entry process is a health check. You must show your passport and the completed forms. If you have listed yellow fever, cholera, venereal disease, leprosy, or tuberculosis, or indicated that you are HIV positive on the health card, you will be denied entry or sent to the airport clinic for further testing. If you are entering from an area that has yellow fever epidemics, you must have a certificate of inoculation.

If you will be spending an extended period of time in China, you will have to have a quarantine certificate issued by an authorized health department. If you are staying in China for six months or longer, you must have an HIV test, which can be given in China or at home. Tests performed at a government facility (i.e., your state's health department) are acceptable; tests performed at a private facility must be notarized. There are specific requirements for documentation, so check with the Chinese embassy or consulate to find out what applies in your situation.

In the next step, border control, you must show the officer your passport, which must have a valid visa and an entry registration card. As a rule, China does not issue visas at the border, so you might be denied entry. In fact, contrary to what most people believe, a visa is merely an application to ask for entry to the country when you arrive; it is in no way a guarantee that you will be permitted entry. You can check with the Chinese consulate or embassy nearest you for the latest information on entry requirements and how to obtain the necessary visa and entry forms. Contact information for embassies and consulates can be found in Appendix B.

Next comes customs. If you have nothing to declare, head for the green area; if you do have items to declare, you must go to the red area. A customs officer will determine if you must pay a duty on any items you are bringing in; gifts that you are bringing into China may be subject to duty taxes. At the officer's discretion you may be forbidden from taking some items in to the country, or you may be warned that you will have to prove when you leave that you are still in possession of valuables brought into China. For example, if you bring your video camera with you, you may be given a form that you will have to produce, along with the camera, when you depart to prove that you have not sold it during your stay. Keep all forms given to you by customs, as you may need to produce them upon your departure. If for some reason you do not take out some of the items you brought in, you may be asked to pay duty on them when you leave.

There are many items that cannot be taken into China, such as weapons. Although most of these forbidden items are obvious, such as illicit drugs, others are not. For example, you may not bring into China any material—printed, audio, video, or any other medium—that is harmful to China's political, economic, cultural, or ethnic life, and you may not take in narcotics. This is at the discretion of the customs officer. It's better not to take with you any magazines or the like than to risk the trouble that can result from something as simple as a magazine article about China, or an ad that may be deemed pornographic, even if it is commonplace in your culture. To minimize trouble regarding narcotics and medicines, be sure that any medication you take with you, including over-the-counter medication, is in its original bottle and clearly labeled. If you have prescription medicines, it is advisable to have a letter from your physician stating what the drug is, including its generic name, and the reason that you must take it.

You can contact the Chinese consulate for further information on arriving in and departing from China. Persons of dual U.S. and Chinese nationality can contact the Office of Overseas Citizens Services at (202) 647–6769 for information about the guidelines for travel to and from China.

If you are planning on being in China for over a month, it's a good idea to register with your embassy or consulate. Registering will facilitate the replacement of lost or stolen passports and make it easier to notify loved ones at home in case of an emergency.

BUSINESS TRIPS TO CHINA

In order to make a business trip to China, you must first have an invitation. In other words, if you would like to find a Chinese supplier, you can't just fly into China and try to set up appointments. But don't let the need for an invitation discourage you; they are relatively easy to obtain. If you already have a business partner in China, you can ask for his company's assistance with the application procedure. If you are new to China, you can explore various trade missions and other opportunities available through international chambers of commerce, trade development organizations, and the Chinese and U.S. governments. Although the process does not cost anything, be sure you leave enough time to get things done. Appendix B lists some resources that can get you started.

LEAVING CHINA

We're getting a bit ahead of ourselves here, but keep in mind that leaving China is somewhat simpler, assuming your paperwork is in order. As mentioned above, forms given to you upon entry must be presented upon departure and you must have the listed items. If an item is missing you must have official documentation explaining why you no longer have the item, such as a police report in the case that something was stolen from you. Otherwise you will probably have to pay an import tax on the missing items.

You will have to pay an exit fee of about 90 yuan. This must be paid in local currency, so be sure you have enough left to cover this cost.

China does have strict laws about exporting, including antiques and cultural relics, medicinal materials, and precious metals. If you have purchased antiques, be sure you have the receipt as proof of purchase. (As you are shopping for antiques, you will see that items that can be exported will have a red wax seal; those that cannot be exported will not.)

You cannot take Chinese currency out of China, even as a souvenir. If you have leftover currency that you want to change back into foreign (non-Chinese) currency at the airport, you will have to show the exchange receipt that was given to you when you initially changed money into renminbi.

The key to a relatively painless arrival and departure, then, is to have all of your documents in order and to keep every receipt or form given to you while you are in China. It can also be helpful to jot down what each piece of paper is for if you don't read Chinese so that you will have an easier time remembering which receipt or form goes with which item.

GETTING AROUND

Now that you've gotten to China, you'll need to know how to get around. China is a very expansive country, and with a population of 1.25 billion people, even a not-so-major city can seem like a megalopolis to us. This section will help you get from Point A to Point B despite all that.

Driving

Rental cars are not available in China. As an alternative, consider hiring a chauffeur driven car or engaging a taxi for a block of time. Chauffeured cars can be hired through the China International Travel Service (CITS) or your hotel. If you are on a business trip, you can probably enlist the aid of your host organization in hiring a car service.

If you are going to be living in China, you may want to consider getting a Chinese driver's license. More information on driving and driver's licenses in China can be found in the chapter titled Living and Staying in China.

Taxis

An easy option in cities is, of course, the taxi. Taxis are generally safe and inexpensive for local travel. You'll have no trouble identifying them. They're usually yellow or red. They have a light on top and the name of the taxi company painted on the side. You can easily hail a taxi on the street. There are also taxi lines that form outside larger hotels, or you can call for a pick up.

It's unlikely that the driver will speak anything other than Chinese, so have someone write down your destination so you can show the driver. Be sure the driver starts the meter when you start your trip. Some small change is sufficient to tip the driver, unless he has helped with your luggage, a service that warrants a somewhat larger tip. Tipping is a sensitive issue in China, so be sure you are discreet about it.

You can hire a car and driver for excursions or for the duration of your stay at reasonable rates. Because of language barriers, this transaction is best negotiated with the help of your hotel concierge or a Chinese colleague.

Public Transportation

Public transportation is widely available and inexpensive, although the level of comfort varies. Flights to major cities within China are readily available, as are trains. Unfortunately, however, the public transportation infrastructure does not always meet the needs of increased travel and tourism, so planes and trains are frequently overbooked.

Trains

The Chinese rail network is extensive, serving all provinces except for Tibet. Trains have four classes: soft berth, hard berth, soft seat,

and hard seat. In soft berth, there are two to four beds in an enclosed compartment. Although soft berth is the most expensive class of ticket, it's advisable for long journeys. Hard berth has six beds per compartment and is not closed; there are seats along the corridor. Soft seat cars are air-conditioned with cushioned seats; these are available only on short distance trains. The least expensive class is hard seat, and as such the cars are usually crowded, with about one hundred seats per car and often with people standing as well.

Train tickets can be difficult to reserve; your hotel or a colleague may be able to assist you. Round-trip tickets are easier-to-purchase from a travel agent. While it's best to purchase your ticket well in advance of your trip, that's not always possible. If the booking agency tells you there are no tickets, you may want to call or stop by the train station to inquire further. Travelers who were told "no" in one place have nevertheless been able to purchase a ticket in the other.

Subway

Both Beijing and Shanghai have extensive subway systems. Subway trains run from 5:30 A.M. to 10:30 P.M. The subway fare is a flat rate no matter how far you are travelling. You can buy your ticket at the ticket booth; tickets are not dated and can be purchased in multiples. Attendants at the platform take your ticket. Platform signs are usually in both Chinese and Pīnyīn (romanized) characters.

Other Options

Many major hotels in large cities offer a bus service to and from the airport and downtown areas.

Bicycles are abundant in China. They are a good means of transportation on the busy streets of big cities. You can rent a bike in one of the many rental shops you will find in most cities.

TRAVEL TIPS

Here are a few miscellaneous points to keep in mind when you're traveling to or through China. You'll find a few of these particularly helpful.

Make a photocopy of the data page of your passport and keep it apart from your passport. If your passport is lost or stolen, you will have the information you need to replace it.

The electric voltage in China is 220 volts/50 Hertz. Outlets have three-connectors (L, N, and E). Some hotels have a 110-volt outlet in the bathroom; this is suitable for electric razors, but not hair dryers.

China uses the metric system of weights and measures. Because many people are accustomed to the traditional Chinese system, you will see a mixture of metric and the traditional Chinese system. See Appendix C for conversion information.

Pay toilets can be found on the street and in tourist places in larger cities at a cost of 20–30 yuan. Toilets in airports and large shopping centers are free of charge. Many Westerners are dismayed to find themselves in a toilet that consists of a porcelain trough in the floor flanked by footpads; one faces the covered end of the trough and squats to use such facilities. Remember, "when in Beijing..." If there is any toilet paper at all, you will probably need to dispose of it in a bin rather than flushing it. It's advisable to carry a packet of tissues.

FIVE

LIVING AND STAYING IN CHINA

If you're not planning on renting or buying a house in China, you may want to skip ahead to Bringing Your Belongings on page 124.

RESIDENCE PERMIT

One of the first things on your to-do list when you move to China will be to obtain a Residence Permit (Green Card). You will need to do this within the first few days. Having your employer apply on your behalf can expedite the process. Once you receive the permit, which is more like a small booklet than card, you will need to have it with you at all times—it's probably more even important than your passport. And try not to lose it, because it is difficult to replace. Make a photocopy of it just in case.

Green cards are issued for one year and must be renewed annually. One of the benefits of having the card (other than the simple fact that you must have one if you will be living in China) is that it entitles you to pay the same fare as locals in hotels, on trains, and for airfare, among other things. China is notorious for having two prices on many things: one for locals and one for foreigners.

HOUSING

Finding housing as a foreigner can be tricky. There are a number of challenges and a number of things you will need to take into consideration, such as where your children will be going to school, the location of your office, the amenities you require, and how you expect to get around town. Therefore it is wise to begin your housing search as early as possible, preferably with a house-hunting trip prior to the actual move.

As a foreigner in China, you may only live in housing especially designated for foreigners. The landlord or management company must hold a Foreign Sales Permit in order to offer housing to foreigners. Most expatriates moving to China choose to rent rather than buy. Rental properties come in a wide variety of quality and price, but most are owned by real estate management companies and hotels.

Foreign housing is usually a compound or mini-community of expatriates, or student dormitories. You can choose from apartments, townhouses, or houses. Apartment complexes are generally closer to the city centers; compounds of single family houses are mostly farther from the hustle and bustle of the city and have more open space. In addition to these options, some hotels offer full-service apartments, giving you the amenities of a hotel with the atmosphere of a home.

Another option to consider is a furnished apartment available

through some hotels and real estate brokers. These apartments usually offer more services, such as laundry and fitness centers, for an additional service fee. Furnished apartments can also be found through a few international apartment service firms (please see Appendix B for contact information), which can arrange accommodations for any length of stay, from a few weeks to long-term relocations.

The quality and size of housing varies considerably, depending on where in China you will be settling. In Beijing, most foreign housing, especially the more recently constructed buildings, are on par with Western standards and most are of comparable size as well. Housing in Shanghai, however, tends to leave something to be desired, and is usually smaller.

You will want to consider carefully what qualities are important to you when you select your new home. Depending on which complex or compound you choose, your mini-community may offer few amenities or it may offer the works: playground, swimming pool, clubhouse, exercise facilities, supermarket, and restaurants. You will want to take into consideration how far you would have to commute to work, keeping in mind that traffic congestion can mean a frustrating and time-consuming commute. If you have children, you will probably want to consider proximity to schools, but you may also be interested in living in a complex that has its own shuttle bus to the schools your children will be attending.

Obviously, the more amenities offered, the more expensive the home. Rent in China is high, compared to the United States; Beijing and Shanghai are both on the list of the five most expensive cities to live in based on rent per square footage.

Finding a Living Space

There are lots of different ways to find a place to live. You can peruse the ads in English-language newspapers, work with a real estate broker specializing in foreign housing, or contact the management companies that run the compounds you are interested in. Newspapers such as the *Beijing Weekend* and *China Daily* have advertising sections. However, since foreign housing is strictly regulated, most of those ads are placed by brokers, not individuals.

Because of the intricacies of locating housing as an expatriate, the majority of expatriates in China enlist the assistance of a real estate broker. Before you select a broker, check the company's background and ensure that they have the necessary business permits. Expect to pay the equivalent of two to three months' rent as the broker's fee.

If you are disappointed by the fact that you will be segregated from the local population, remember that it is illegal for foreigners to live in housing designated for locals, unless they are married to a Chinese person. There is the very real possibility, if you do rent local housing, that you will be evicted by the authorities; if this happens, don't expect to get back any deposits or rent paid to the landlord.

Moving In

Renters will need to pay a deposit and have a contract. You will probably have to pay two to three months' rent in advance, as well as a security deposit. The deposit can range from one to three months' rent. As with any contract, it is advisable to speak with someone knowledgeable about the local environment before signing. Be sure you have had your rights and responsibilities, including any additional fees, clearly explained before entering into a rental or lease agreement.

People moving to other countries have again and again been caught off guard when it came time to move into their new, unfurnished homes. If your living space was inhabited when you first looked at it (if you even had the opportunity to see it in advance at all), you may have assumed that some of the items you saw there came with the apartment. Many a new tenant has found himself or herself without a refrigerator or even lights upon moving in because those things belonged to the previous tenants, who naturally took them when they left. Generally speaking, an unfurnished apartment guarantees you nothing more than four solid walls, a floor and a ceiling. Appliances that most American renters find in unfurnished apartments, such as a refrigerator, are not necessarily part of the deal in China. Therefore it is important that you clarify exactly what will be in the apartment when you move in, down to the fixtures.

This is important if you are moving into a furnished apartment as well. Don't expect to find the full range of home appliances, such as a microwave oven or washing machine, even in a furnished apartment. A furnished apartment should come complete with pots and pans, utensils, and bedding, though.

Other details to discuss with your potential landlord before committing to a contract are the availability of telephone lines, utilities (gas and electricity), hot water, heat, and air-conditioning.

It is advisable to rent a house or apartment that already has telephone service whenever possible. Applying for a new telephone number is quite expensive (approximately $300–$400) and can take several months to acquire. Fortunately, most expatriate housing is already equipped with telephone lines, heat, air-conditioning, and twenty-four-hour hot water availability. However, it is wiser not to take anything for granted and verify every detail.

Heat is usually included in your monthly rent, but utilities and telephone charges are not. These are generally paid at an on-site accounting office or to the landlord. Again, you should find out in advance what you will be charged for these amenities, since some landlords tack a "service charge" onto the actual rate. In addition to utility and telephone, you may have to pay a management fee, usually around 5% of your rent.

Buying Property

If you wish to buy property in China, you will need a Foreign Sales Permit. Your options for buying are limited to those properties designated for foreigners. A real estate agent can help you locate available properties. It's advisable to make sure that everything is in order before signing the papers, which will be written in Mandarin.

BRINGING YOUR BELONGINGS

There is a steep duty on imported furniture in China, so you will need to put some thought into what you will bring with you. There are additional considerations, including whether or not your furniture will fit your new home, what appliances will and will not work in China, and the range of products that are readily available in China.

Because moving to China can be an overwhelming experience, many families prefer to stock up on the items they use most, such as disposable diapers and baby formula, personal care products, and food items, before moving. This allows some breathing room to locate stores that carry the products they need or find suitable substitutes.

Appliances and Computers

Electricity in China is 220 volts/50 Hertz, compared to the 110 volts/60 Hertz used in the United States. Most American appliances, therefore will not work without a current transformer. In addition, appliances such as refrigerators, air-conditioners, clocks, microwaves, vacuum cleaners, and stereos will not work properly, even with a transformer, because of the difference in Hertz. China has a variety of plug shapes. Your outlets might take three-prong, round pin, parallel flat pin, or angled flat pin plugs. If you are taking over any of your own appliances, check to see what type of outlets your home has; you will need the plug adapter for each appliance.

There are several options for obtaining appliances. You will first want to see what, if any, appliances come with your house or apartment. If you need other appliances, you can, of course, buy them locally. However, there are other alternatives. For example, you can look into buying them from other people who are leaving the country (many compounds have a bulletin board or a newsletter for this type of thing). There are also companies that specialize in providing appliances to people moving overseas that meet the local requirements. Some of these companies are listed in Appendix B.

More and more companies offer Internet service. In Beijing, you can expect to pay about RMB300 (approximately $35) per month for unlimited Internet access. However, you will also have to pay a connection charge for the telephone call; the rates are the same as a regular phone call.

Several Western companies such as AOL and CompuServe operate in China, or you can choose a local Internet Service Provider. Local ISPs are government run and are subject to censorship. You will need to ask if your computer needs any kind of special configuration for Chinese characters. Don't forget to verify that the telephone line is digital before using your modem, especially if you are in a hotel. You risk damaging the computer if the line is analog.

UTILITIES

Electricity in China is subject to brownouts, sometimes with advance warning, sometimes without. Some expatriate compounds have a backup power generator. If yours does not, having your own can be handy. In any case, a surge protector and uninterrupted backup power supply for your computer is a must.

Water shortages also occur occasionally, although expatriates who live in foreign compounds are not likely to experience this. Some areas can go days or even weeks without access to water.

By the Way...

ENVIRONMENTAL CONCERNS

Pollution is a serious problem in China. Almost 70% of China's energy needs are met with coal. Continued economic growth means more pollution as more and more cars hit China's streets and more homes are constructed. Unfortunately, China's infrastructure is poorly equipped to handle the burden, and energy cannot be consumed efficiently. Exacerbating the problem is the fact that the coal industry is heavily subsidized, making it the most cost-efficient source of fuel, a big incentive to keep using coal. Consequently, coal burning continues to wreak havoc on China's environment.

TELEPHONES

Less than 40% of the people in China have a private telephone in their home. There are two types of telephone lines: domestic and international (IDD). An IDD line is necessary to direct dial international calls. In the event that the phone you are using does not have an IDD line, you can dial the international operator at 115 to place the call. Cellular phones and pagers offer a cost-efficient alternative to landlines, and the number of subscribers to both is increasing rapidly.

Luckily, most expatriate housing comes equipped with telephones already installed, both domestic and IDD. If you need to have a line installed—such as an extra line for a fax or modem—and you live in a compound for foreigners, you can probably just ask the management company since many have extra lines available.

In the unfortunate event that you do need to have a new telephone line installed by the Ministry of Post and Telecommunications (MPT), you should gird yourself for a frustrating time. It can take as much as three months to have a line installed. You will need to apply at the MPT and pay the applicable fees, which are about 5,000 yuan for a private line and 15,000 yuan for a personal line. Don't forget to specify that you also need an IDD line, which will cost an additional 3,000 yuan or so.

If you wish to buy a cellular phone, you will find that the cellular networks are reliable. Several companies offer cellular service; however, you will have to sign up with a provider when you buy the telephone. Pagers are available through a number of companies.

All calls, local or long-distance, are toll calls. The charge is calculated based on the length of the call for local calls and the length and distance for long distance calls. Hotels often charge a hefty surcharge for international calls.

You can make local or long-distance (but usually not international) calls from the public pay phones or privately-owned "public" phones that entrepreneurial locals have set up on virtually every corner. Most larger hotels have public phones in the lobby and there are telecommunications centers located throughout the city. Phones and phone booths are indicated by red signs. Booths often have several phones with an attendant to monitor charges and make change. To use the phone, dial the number, then push the green button when your party answers. Local calls are 5 jiao or 1 yuan for three minutes.

There are three types of public phones: coin operated, magnetic card operated, and "Smartcard" operated. The magnetic card phones are being phased out in favor of Smartcard phones, since they can be easily remagnitized illegally. Smartcards are not easily defrauded. Prepaid phone cards are issued by the MPT and as well as by other companies. You can purchase phone cards at the post office, in hotels and in some shops. The magnetic phone cards are valid only for calls within the province where they were purchased; Smartcards work anywhere in China. Phone card calls are generally slightly cheaper than coin calls, since you do not have to pay the three minute minimum.

If you need to make an international call you will need to go to a telecommunications center, which is usually located in or near the city's main post office. The centers are open twenty-four hours a day. To make the call, pay the deposit at the cashier, who will assign you a booth. After you have completed your call(s) you will pay the cashier for all calls. International telephone rates from China to the United States are much higher than from the United States to China; whenever possible, have colleagues, family, and friends call you.

Telephone Tips

- Telegraph offices, the post office, and major hotels (you don't need to be a guest) often offer fax and Telex service.
- The most common way to answer the telephone is "*Wei, wei*" (pronounced "way").
- Finding a place to plug in your modem when you are traveling can be problematic. However, many four- and five-star hotels do have this amenity available. Be sure to ask if the line is digital; you could ruin your computer if you try to use the modem on an analog line.

Useful Phone Numbers

The following numbers are the same throughout China. Unfortunately, however, except for international assistance, it is unlikely that the person who answers the phone will speak English.

Police: 110
Fire: 119
Ambulance/Medical emergency: 120
Local directory assistance: 114
Long-distance assistance: 113 or 173
International assistance: 115
Information: 114 (in Chinese)

PETS

It's quite difficult and expensive to bring a pet into China. Dogs are especially difficult. A dog is required to have a "Residence for Dog" permit and must meet certain health requirements. Most dogs and cats are subject to quarantine; the exact requirements depend on the species.

The regulations on pet importation are confusing and can be changed at short notice. Before deciding to bring your pet with you,

contact the Chinese embassy or consulate (see Appendix B) for regulations and details about bringing your animal into China.

In general, your pet must have routine immunizations at least 35 days, but not more than 180 days, prior to arrival. The pet is also required to have a Health Certificate with export endorsement issued by the U.S. Department of Agriculture or another equivalent organization within ten days of departure. An original rabies certificate from your vet, signed in ink, must accompany the Health Certificate. Color photographs of your pet, taken from all sides, may also be required.

Once you have arrived in China with Fido, you will find that he is unfortunately not welcome in many places. For example, Beijing has a limit to the size of dog you may have; only small dogs are permitted. Dogs must be walked between 8:00 P.M. and 7:00 A.M., and are banned from markets, parks, hotels and several other public places. Pets such as cats or fish are easier to keep in China.

Pets are not as common in China as in the United States, so products and services (veterinary, grooming, etc.) are relatively difficult to come by. If your pet requires any special medication or food be sure to bring an adequate supply with you. If you will be making a preliminary trip to China, make a note to check to see if your pet's needs can be met.

BRINGING YOUR VEHICLE

There are many restrictions on importing vehicles into China. Because the regulations are set by province, it is impossible to give a full picture. However, there is generally an import limit of one vehicle per family allowed, as well as size restrictions, and applicable taxes. As is usually the case, regulations are subject to change without notice, so you will need to contact the Chinese consulate or embassy for current details.

The price of automobiles in China is about twice that of U.S. prices, although purchasing a domestically produced vehicle can save you a bit of money. There are many alternative means of transportation, some of which can be more expedient than driving, due to heavy traffic in the cities. Other popular modes of transportation are bicycles, public transportation such as minibuses (which are more comfortable than regular city buses), and the subway. You can also call a cab or even rent a car as necessary. Refer back to the "Getting Around" section for more details. However, if you work in remote, less developed cities, it is usually preferable to have your own car.

Getting a Driver's License

If you intend to drive in China, you will need a Chinese driver's license (*Jiàshǐ Zhízhào*). Before you go, find out what policies your company has regarding ownership of vehicles and driving in China. Many companies do not allow expatriates to drive because of potential insurance and legal issues.

You must apply for a driver's license at the Foreigners Division of Vehicles in Beijing. In order to get a license, you need proof of your job, a residence permit, and a driver's license from your home country. You will then need to get a health exam and have the applicable section of the application filled out by the doctor. Then you must have your employer fill out another section of the application, after which you return the completed application to the Foreigners Division of Vehicles, accompanied by your passport, photos, and your home-country license. Your home-country license will be kept by the Public Security Bureau until you surrender your Chinese license at your departure.

SCHOOLS

While there are several international schools in Beijing and at least one in most other major cities, the majority of these schools have a waiting list. It is therefore advisable to get your child on the waiting list of the school you choose as soon as possible. You should also consider putting your child on the waiting list of alternate choices, should the first choice not become available.

You will need to research the schools that will be available in your area to determine which one is suitable for your child. Curricula can vary according to the school's affiliation. The age of your child and the length of your stay will both be factors in your decision. For example, an older child who will be returning home for college needs a curriculum that will allow him or her to stay on track for college entry.

If your child is quite young and will be able to pick up Chinese fairly quickly, you might want to consider placing him or her in a Chinese school. Many schools have special programs for foreigners and concentrate on learning Chinese and a few other subjects. There are both advantages and disadvantages to this choice. It can be a very positive experience for your child, and will obviously allow him or her to learn the Chinese language and culture, as well as get an early, accelerated introduction to math. The most obvious drawback is the lack of English language and other subjects, such as American history, that would be received at an American school. Home schooling and boarding schools are other options to consider. While researching schools, you will want to take into account the following:

- Is the curriculum appropriate?
- Will your child be prepared to reenter the American educational system upon returning home?
- What type of environment will your child benefit most from in terms of language of instruction, teaching methods, and interaction with other children?
- What is the school's accreditation and recognition, both in China and in your home country?
- What quality of education does the school offer in terms of teacher qualifications, class size, and teaching material?

SHOPPING

Where to Shop

China offers a wide variety of places to shop, from large shopping malls to open-air markets. In large cities you will find department stores and supermarkets. Your best bet for finding imported food and personal care products in the largest supermarkets, such as Friendship Stores and Wellcome Supermarkets, which are found in larger cities. In recent years, more and more large foreign stores have opened in large cities. Wal-Mart has warehouses in Shenzhen, while Shanghai has the Yashan department store (Japanese), Shanghai Jusco (Japanese), and Biko and Tops (Singapore).

There are also smaller stores where you can shop for daily needs such as baked goods, meat, vegetables, and common items such as shampoo or detergent. Convenience stores mainly sell snack foods and sodas, cigarettes, etc. Open-air markets are open seven days a week. Here you can buy fresh fruit and vegetables, meat, fish, eggs, and more.

You can use foreign currency in Friendship Stores, located in most larger cities. This chain of stores was the government's method of both pleasing and isolating foreigners. The stores carry scarce and foreign goods that are not readily available to the general population and originally served only foreigners. Friendship Stores generally carry a wide range of items, including imported goods, ranging from food to appliances to home decorations. Nowadays in China, however, you will most likely find the same wide array of consumer goods in other Chinese department stores as well.

China is a cash society. However, many larger department stores now accept credit and debit cards. It should be noted that foreigners are often overcharged on everything from travel tickets to produce.

You can test your haggling skills to bargain for the best prices in shops and at markets; in fact, it's expected. But don't try it in department stores where the prices are clearly marked. Keep in mind, however, that bargaining is neither a test of wills nor an exercise in intimidation. Either of those approaches is likely to net a higher price, not a lower one. Bargaining should be an exchange where both the merchant and the customer are able to maintain their face by reaching a mutually acceptable price. It might be a polite conversation or a small drama in two acts, beginning with much throwing up of one's arms and fulsome phrases of hyperbole, followed by the real negotiation. Make your goal talking your way down to a price that a local would pay instead of the "foreigner's price."

Drug stores can provide you with a wide range of medicines and remedies over-the-counter, as well as personal care products. Generally speaking, there are more items available without a doctor's prescription than in the United States. It is a good idea to keep a list of the generic names of any particular medicines you take.

Stores are generally open between 9:00 A.M. and 8:30 P.M. Most stores are closed only three days a year, during the Spring Festival (Chinese New Year).

Because the cuisine of China is so different from Western cuisine, you may find it challenging to locate your family's favorite foods. Items such as cereal, frozen pizza, pretzels, and so on are hard to come by. Your best bet is to try the largest supermarket in the city or a store in an expatriate compound. If you are in a smaller city or rural area, shopping is more difficult. Food and consumer goods are scarcer and the likelihood of finding Western goods is almost nil. Of course, if you're willing to readjust your taste buds and culinary comfort zone, you'll be more than satisfied.

One final note: don't expect to be able to pick up a few items at your local gas station. Unlike the United States, where many gas stations carry convenience items, such as soda, cigarettes and even groceries, gas is the only commodity available at a Chinese gas station.

The Western style of clothing prevails in China. However, you will probably notice that there are more bright colors than you would see in the United States. The selection of clothing for children is somewhat limited, especially for infants and toddlers. Your older children may not care for the clothes available to them, since the current trends in teen fashion are not available.

A common complaint heard from Westerners is that it can be difficult to find clothes that fit, since the average Chinese is smaller than the average American. This is especially true if you wear larger sizes or are above average height. The good news is that tailors abound and you can have clothes made to fit you at reasonable prices. Ask around for recommendations for a tailor. You can even take in a favorite blouse or pair of pants and have the tailor make one just like it. Shoes that fit a Westerner's foot, however, are notoriously difficult to come by. It's not a good idea to rely on finding a pair in China.

Many Americans are used to the idea that you can return virtually any item for a refund or exchange. In fact, some people make it a habit to shop "on spec," especially for items such as clothing. In the United States, if it turns out that the shirt didn't match the pants like you thought it would, you can just return the shirt to the store and try again. Once you arrive in China, you will have to change that mindset. Items, once purchased, are generally not returnable unless they are defective. In that case, the item may be exchanged, but not refunded.

Putting items on sale is another phenomenon that is largely limited to within North American borders. Chinese stores offer sales only at the end of seasons and before a few holidays.

Service

Service with a smile is a concept that is just beginning to make headroads in China. Increased competition has more managers encouraging their staff to work more efficiently and even to be more friendly. However, *méiyǒu* is still a refrain often heard. *Méiyǒu* is a phrase that literally means "don't have," but the person's tone of voice and demeanor will tell you if he or she really means "I don't want to bother to look," or "Go away."

The quality of service is notoriously poor when it comes to government officials, who view their ability to make supplicants wait as a matter of face. In contrast, the service in privately owned shops and businesses is generally quick and friendly.

FINANCIAL MATTERS

China's currency is the renminbi (RMB). The basic unit of RMB is the yuan. 10 jiao=1 yuan; 10 fen=1 jiao. Paper notes come in denominations of 100, 50, 10, 5, 2, and 1 yuan; 5, 2, and 1 jiao; and 5, 2, and 1 fen. Coin denominations are 1 yuan; 5, 2, and 1 jiao; and 5, 2, and 1 fen.

Cash is necessary to get by in China. Personal checks are not accepted; credit cards can be used only in major hotels and restaurants and some shopping centers. You will probably have to pay about a 4% surcharge for using a credit card.

You can change money and traveler's checks at authorized banks, such as the Bank of China, in airports, and in some of the bigger hotels and department stores. Some of the shopping malls that are frequented by foreigners also offer currency conversion service. When you change your money, ask for a receipt, which you may need to facilitate the conversion of leftover RMB back to your currency before leaving China.

Although black market currency exchange is forbidden, you may be approached by people offering to change your money at a higher rate than the bank offers. It is best not to accept, as you risk being caught in an illegal activity or being cheated with counterfeit currency.

Personal Banking

As a foreigner, you may only open a checking accounts at an authorized bank. The Bank of China is authorized to open accounts for foreigners residing throughout China and offers the most service for international customers. In larger cities such as Beijing and Shanghai, a handful of other banks are authorized to hold foreigner's accounts.

Government regulations require that expatriate employees of foreign-invested companies be paid in foreign currency, which can be the cause of many a headache. While you can open a foreign-currency account at the Bank of China, the services offered for these accounts can be agonizingly slow. A check drawn on your foreign currency account can take months to clear. Many expatriates elect to be paid in cash, by direct deposit to an account in their home country, or a combination of the two. Funds in the home account can usually then be accessed by a Visa debit card or by personal check (if you have an American Express card to guarantee it). If you have made arrangements for paying your credit card bills from home (many banks with special accounts for expatriates offer this services, as do some accountants specializing in expatriate matters), you can use most major credit cards to get cash. Obviously these services carry fees, depending on the policy of your financial institution. However, they are often the most viable alternative to a foreign currency account.

While most banks are open every day in most major cities, foreign exchange is available only on weekdays during certain business hours. One of the first things on your "to do" list is to find out the necessary information from your local branch.

The most popular type of account in China is the passbook savings account. Expatriates coming from an increasingly cashless society like the United States will have to readjust their thinking. Most everyday transactions in China are cash only. If you are used to paying with a credit card at the gas station, grocery store, and in restaurants, you will have to change your mindset. While some larger department stores will accept a credit or debit card, most will not. Hotels, restaurants, and stores that cater to foreigners are more likely to accept credit cards, but it's a good idea to check first.

The use of checks is also uncommon except for large-ticket items. Bills are generally paid by bank transfer, not by check. ATMs, while not available on every street corner, are becoming increasingly available in large cities. However, if you are traveling outside of larger cities, ATMs are scarce to nonexistent. Some ATMs will accept debit cards on the Plus system.

If you should lose a major credit card (Visa, Mastercard, American Express, Diner's Club, etc.) while in China, go to a Bank of China branch to arrange for a replacement.

SOCIALIZING

Anger is more harmful than
the insult that caused it.

—Chinese proverb

Meeting People and Making Friends

There are several facts that make it difficult for expatriates to interact with the Chinese community. The greatest hurdle is the relative
isolation of foreigners, who are allowed to live only in certain places,
set aside and away from the local population. A second factor is the
fact that Chinese society—and therefore much of the leisure activity—revolves largely around family. All of these factors combine to
make it difficult for foreigners to make Chinese friends. In most
cases, office relationships do not extend beyond working hours, and
since business entertaining does not usually include family, your
spouse and your colleagues' spouses may never meet.

If you do make a personal connection with a Chinese coworker,
it is unlikely that you will be invited to that person's home, as the
Chinese do not as a rule entertain at home. In addition, he or she
may not be comfortable coming to your home alone, so you will

probably find yourself enjoying each other's company in a restaurant for dinner and karaoke.

This feeling of isolation can be very difficult, and is especially hard on accompanying partners. It is extremely difficult for accompanying partners to obtain a work permit; if they are lucky enough to do so, it is generally for positions such as English teacher.

Most nonworking expatriates in China therefore find a way to use their skills and develop their interests within the expatriate community. Opportunities for social activities abound, as do athletic clubs, entertainment venues, and more. Many people find a way to "work" in China by volunteering their services in some way. If you are interested in finding a niche for yourself, you can ask around at your children's school or contact an expatriate club or organization where you are interested in being involved.

Chinese generally work long hours and many spend a great deal of time each day commuting long distances to their jobs. As a result, they don't have a lot of leisure time. While organized sports are not common, many Chinese enjoy table tennis and badminton, which they play during their extended lunch breaks and on weekends. Unfortunately, China does not offer a wide variety of leisure-time activities. In larger cities there are theaters, nightclubs, and so on, although little of it is geared toward non-Chinese speakers. Things are changing very rapidly in big cities such as Beijing and Shanghai. In Beijing, you can go to San Wei Shu Wu where they sell books during the day, serve coffee and tea upstairs, and even have a Chinese-American band playing there. The crowd is a mixture of Chinese and foreigners. You can also go to a restaurant called "Half and Half," where foreigners mingle with Chinese. Shanghai Waitan also has gathering places similar to these.

If you want to interact with Chinese people, try going to your local park, where you are likely to find table tennis and badminton nets. In general, the best way to meet people is to do something that you like to do. A photography buff with a camera around his neck may find himself striking up a conversation with other picture takers, a painter may find that her easel draws some attention.

The Chinese generally prefer to go out in large groups and don't value privacy as much as Westerners. Many expatriates have a had a tough time explaining to their Chinese friends that they would like to spend some time alone without hurting anyone's feelings!

Be My Guest: Being on Your Best Behavior as a Host or Guest

If you wish to entertain your Chinese friends or colleagues, it is best to invite them as part of a group. Although most Chinese do not entertain at home, except for very close friends, you can feel free to host a dinner or party. If you live in a compound for foreigners, your Chinese guests might be questioned by the authorities and have their name taken, even if you have given them a printed invitation. Some may decline an invitation for that reason. This is most likely to happen in small cities in remote areas.

An invitation to a Chinese home is a rare thing and should be treated as the honor it is. It may be many years, if ever, before an invitation is extended. Until a personal relationship is established, most Chinese prefer to entertain in restaurants. If you are invited to a Chinese home, you will be the center of attention. This is a social occasion, so don't talk business. Don't be surprised if your hosts have invited relatives, friends, and neighbors to drop by to meet the foreigner.

Take a small gift or flowers with you (but not cut flowers, as to some people, these may symbolize funerals and death). When you arrive, your host may require that you either remove your shoes or change into a pair of indoor shoes or slippers, which can be found near the door. Tea will be served immediately, most likely accompanied by a variety of snacks. Don't eat too many munchies, because a full meal is probably scheduled.

Don't ask for a tour of your hosts' home if one is not offered. Don't be overly admiring of or overly interested in the belongings in a Chinese home; doing so may result in your host offering the item to you as a gift and put both of you in a difficult position. It's better to stick to compliments about the home in general.

Two final notes on Chinese homes. China has a severe shortage of housing. As a consequence, Chinese homes are generally smaller and more crowded than American homes. And while it is no longer forbidden for a foreigner to stay overnight in a Chinese home, a permit from the local police station is required.

Dating and Beyond

If you're single and find yourself in a position to date while you're in China, there are naturally a few things you should keep in mind. In recent years dating customs have relaxed. In the past, Chinese and foreigners were not allowed to form romantic liaisons. Although there has been some liberalization in this area, particularly in the younger generation where interracial marriages have increased dramatically in the last few years, there are still many challenges for interracial couples, not the least of which is pressure from family.

Single people in China must be aware that Chinese attitudes toward dating and sex most likely differ from those in their home country. China has much more traditional ideas about both than most Americans and Europeans. For example, sex before marriage is not as common as in other countries. It is, in fact, against the law for unmarried couples, local or foreign, to have sexual relations. If an unmarried couple is found sharing a room, there will be at minimum a fine to pay; a jail sentence is also possible. Dating couples, no matter what nationality, should observe the local customs and laws that apply. That goes for non-romantic meetings between two people of opposite genders as well. It is more prudent for a man and woman to meet in the office or in a public area of the hotel than for one to go to the other's room, even if they are only discussing business.

Couples do not usually engage in public displays of affection. They don't hug or kiss in public, even in greeting or leave taking. This is changing, however, so you might see younger couples being more casual in displaying affection.

Weddings

Given China's immense history and the fifty-six ethnic groups encompassed in its boundaries, it should come as no surprise that wedding traditions vary from area to area. While weddings in the cities are coming more and more to resemble Western weddings, a common thread is the Three Letters and Six Rituals, summarized below. The preparation for the wedding, the ceremony itself, and the post-ceremony events are also complicated and steeped in tradition.

Historically, the goal of a marriage was the joining and strengthening of two families, and the incorporation of the bride into the groom's family. Marriages were—and sometimes still are—arranged. Therefore, the most important players in the marriage arrangements were the parents, not the bride and groom themselves. The criteria for choosing a bride varied depending on the wealth and status of the groom's family. For a wealthy family, the important thing was that the bride bear many sons to continue the family (though this is no longer

true in China). For a poorer family, it was critical that the bride be able to work hard to contribute to the family's livelihood and to give birth to many sons who would also help out. Under the circumstances, wealthy families invariably sought to marry their sons to the daughters of other wealthy families, while the daughters of poor families married into a family of similar standing.

Although wealth and social status may still play a very important role in choosing a mate, education, character, and personality are increasingly more important to the younger generation. Parents may still try to arrange a relationship, but more often it is classmates, co-workers, teachers, and friends who will play "matchmaker."

The wedding negotiations and the ceremony itself were matters of great formality. Even today, most marriages incorporate the traditions handed down from generations ago.

The Three Letters

Before the advent of modern telecommunications, letters were naturally the primary means of communication. The wedding negotiating included three very important letters:

- The Request Letter, sent from the groom's family to the bride's family, formalizes the wedding agreement.
- The Gift Letter accompanies the formal gifts to the bride's family, listing and describing each gift.
- The Wedding Letter is given to the bride's family on the day of the wedding itself, confirming that the bride has formally become a part of the groom's family.

The Six Rituals

- The request for marriage is made through a spokeswoman when a man has decided on the woman he wants to marry, who acts as a go-between during the initial negotiations.
- Upon the conclusion of the preliminary negotiations, there is a request for the bride and groom's birth dates. A *fēng shǔi*

expert will be hired to determine, based on the birth dates, if the potential bride and groom are a match. If the match is found to be unsuitable, the groom must look for a different woman to marry.

- If the match is deemed suitable by the *feng shui*[4] expert, the groom's family will send the bride's family gifts via the spokeswoman.
- Formal gifts are then sent, confirming the marriage agreement.
- The families will then once again consult a fortune-teller to select an auspicious day for the wedding ceremony.
- On the day of the wedding, the groom's house is decorated in red. The groom's family sends out an entourage of servants and musicians with a carriage to the bride's home. Because the bride's feet may not touch the ground before she reaches the groom's home, the spokeswoman carries the bride on her back to the carriage. The bride is brought to the groom's home, where the two perform the marriage ceremony in front of family and friends.

Prior to the wedding, both bride and groom have gone through a series of rituals in preparation. These include setting up the bridal bed, exchanging gifts, and a ceremonial dressing of the hair of both the bride and groom.

Red is the color of joy and the color of the bride's dress and the veil that covers her face. The wedding ceremony consists of a series of small rituals where the bride and groom pay homage to Heaven and Earth, to their ancestors, and to each other. They then serve tea to all of their elders in their families and in turn receive gifts, usually money enclosed in a red envelope, and good wishes from family members. The groom's family then hosts the celebration with a feast, large or small according to the family's means.

Following the feast, the bride and groom are accompanied to the bridal chamber by friends, where they are often the victims of pranks

[4] For more information see the *Feng Shui* section in the Culture chapter.

played by friends. There they are toasted by the spokeswoman, who wishes them long life and many children until they are finally left alone.

The bride is expected to return to her home three days after the wedding, bearing gifts from the groom's family. In the past this was often the bride's last visit with her family for a long time, since she has now become a member of her husband's family.

Many couples today combine the traditional wedding customs with modern religious and civil ceremonies. The wedding banquet in particular has survived, even where other traditions have not. Another abiding tradition is the selection of auspicious dates for all stages of the process by a *feng shui* expert.

ETIQUETTE

General

If you are introduced to a group of people (for example, if you tour a factory), you may be greeted with applause. You should also clap in greeting. While bows are the standard greeting, you may see handshakes, especially with foreigners. When greeting someone, follow his or her lead. Men can wait for a Chinese to offer his hand for a handshake or bow in reply to his bow. Women who want to shake hands will generally have to offer their hands first. A Chinese handshake is generally quite soft; don't use your power handshake or pump the other person's hand. You will not see people kissing hello or good-bye.

You may see people of the same gender holding hands; this is merely a sign of close friendship. However, it's unlikely that your Chinese friends will do this with you. Queuing is not common; be prepared to assert yourself in stores, at bus stops, and in post offices.

Expect to be stared at when you are out and about. Most Chinese are extremely curious about Westerners and staring is not considered rude. Privacy and personal space are not held sacred. If your Chinese counterpart stands closer to you than is comfortable, try not to back away, since doing so will send a negative signal.

On a personal level, physical contact between strangers is not appreciated. Don't try to pat someone on the back, or casually touch someone's arm. On an impersonal level, such as in crowded subways, buses or trains, contact with others cannot be avoided and there is much pushing and shoving. No apology is necessary in these instances. Because it is forbidden for monks and Buddhist priests to have any physical contact with women, women should take care not to bump into or accidentally brush against them.

Chinese prefer not to display their emotions in public, either verbally or nonverbally. If you are prone to animated gesturing and facial expressions, try to minimize them when speaking with Chinese.

It's considered unclean to put your fingers in your mouth for any reason, so don't lick your fingers! When visiting someone, keep your feet on the floor and off desks, tables, and other furniture.

Your posture is a reflection of your upbringing and education. Don't slouch, and keep both feet on the floor; don't cross your legs. If you need to point, use your open hand, not one finger, which is rude. Never use your head or foot to point out a person. Don't offend by beckoning someone with one finger. Use your whole hand, palm down, and make a scratching motion with your fingers. Don't use your foot to move objects.

Spitting on the sidewalk is common in some parts of China, but it is definitely not good manners. You will also see people blowing their noses (without a tissue) onto the street.

"Going Dutch" does not translate into Chinese. If a colleague or friend pays for a meal or even a subway ride, try to pick up the tab the next time.

Ask for permission before taking pictures of a person. Respect your surroundings in terms of dress, decorum, and photography.

Communicating

Chinese names have the family name first, the given names second. Therefore, Kai Chong Chen's family name is "Kai" and his given name is "Chong Chen." First names are used only by family and close friends. Always address people by their last names and courtesy title (Miss Xie, Mr. Man, etc.). Use professional titles, such as

Doctor, if you know it. Doctor, Mayor, Lawyer, and Professor are professional titles often heard. You will also hear business titles, such as General Manager, Manager, and Engineer. The title can be used without a family name. Do not address someone as Comrade.

Women do not take their husband's name when they marry. Refer to married women by Madam and their own last name. The Chinese sometimes attach affectionate titles to the names of close friends or business associates. For example, *lǎo* (old) may be added to the name of your superior, if you know him well enough. You should not address people with those names unless you are very close. The opposite of *lǎo* is *xiǎo* (young). These terms do not apply in family situations; this usually happens in work places or business relations when you have gained the familiarity or closeness with someone. You use *lǎo* when you assume the person is older or higher in rank, to show respect. You use *xiǎo* when you think the person is younger, to show affection.

Don't be surprised if you are asked questions you wouldn't be asked at home, such as "How old are you?," "Are you married?," and even "How much money do you earn?" Don't be offended by these questions. If you do not wish to answer, you reply, in a friendly tone, with humor. For example, to the question about your income, you might say, "Just enough to pay the bills, I'm afraid." Do not say how much you make without also mentioning the cost of living in your home country. A U.S.-based gross salary is generally several times that of a Chinese salary and you run the risk of alienating co-workers if they perceive only the difference in salary without appreciating the difference in the cost of living.

There are many things that you will enjoy discussing with Chinese, such as travel, cuisine, art, and family. However, some topics are better left alone, such as politics and government (including the situation with Taiwan) and human rights. Other sensitive issues, such as the 1999 U.S. bombing of the Chinese embassy in Belgrade or the charges of espionage on the part of China, are perhaps best left unaddressed. Above all, avoid negative comments about China and its history. No one likes to have his or her country criticized by outsiders. It is best to avoid asking people to express their opinions on the Chinese government; you, in turn, should avoid critical statements about your own government.

Certain gestures and other forms of nonverbal communication are important to know. For example, a laugh or smile is often used to indicate embarrassment or nervousness rather than amusement. A typical expression of displeasure is a quick sucking of air between the teeth. A nod does not always signal agreement. It can be a confirmation that the person has understood you or even a polite gesture if the person has not.

You will have to learn to read between the lines. Chinese are generally uncomfortable communicating negatives, and may respond with a positive to maintain harmony. Negatives might also be communicated in a jesting manner. Humility, patience, and an easygoing nature are all important qualities. Using these skills will ensure harmony, the goal of most interactions. Don't forget the all-important concept of face!

Jokes do not travel well. Puns and double entendres don't translate and references to events or icons of one's home country are often not understood. Avoid sexual or political jokes especially. Avoid the American propensity to start a presentation with a joke to break the ice.

GIFTS

Gift giving is an important part of the Chinese culture, and everything from the gift itself to the wrapping has significance. There are many occasions appropriate for gift giving. For example, at an initial meeting, you should expect to give a modest gift. A gift such as an illustrated book of your state or country may be given to the group, in which case it is presented to the leader. Your gift will most likely be proudly and prominently displayed at the company's offices. A smaller, token gift such as pens with your company logo may be given to each member of the group. If you are giving individual gifts, no one gift should be of greater value, as this will only embarrass the recipient. A gift of greater value is usually given at the conclusion of a business transaction. The same rules of a group or individual gift apply.

Keep in mind that bribery is illegal in China and any gifts you give should be such that they cannot be mistaken for a bribe. Gift giving also creates an obligation to the recipient. Therefore, it is more prudent to accept and give gifts on behalf of your company, where no personal obligation can be attached.

There is a certain protocol to keep in mind for the actual acceptance and giving of gifts. Give and receive gifts with both hands. In order not to appear greedy, it is appropriate to decline the gift a few times before accepting it. Be prepared to gently "insist" that your gift be accepted, and humbly decline a gift offered to you. As a rule of thumb, you might accept the gift on the third offering. Gifts are not opened in the presence of the giver. Do not insist that your gifts be opened, and wait until later to open gifts given to you.

Wrapping is also important. Gifts should be simply but elegantly wrapped, although the wrapping should not be more opulent than the gift. You can ask for wrapping assistance from the store clerk (if you purchased it in China) or the hotel concierge. It is not necessary to enclose a card with the gift. The color of the wrapping paper is very important. Red has good connotations, as do pink and yellow. On the other hand, avoid white, black or blue, as these colors are associated with death. Numbers are also important. Among Cantonese speaking people, four is an unlucky number (because the word "four" in Chinese is similar to the word "death"); eight is particularly lucky. Two and six are also good numbers. Therefore you should avoid giving, for example, a set of four golf balls or even two pairs of something. One is also not a good number, so most people give two items. For example, you might bring two boxes of cookies to your host's home.

Customs officials may want to inspect items brought with you to China, so it's better to bring them unwrapped and wrap them when you get there.

Appropriate business gifts may be pens, paperweights, or other items with your company logo, high-quality whiskey or brandy, illustrated books of your country, or items that are typical of your country. Gifts that show genuine thought and foresight are better than a last-minute purchase from the duty-free shop. Use the knowledge you have gained about your Chinese colleague's interests and family. Does his or her child excel in English? Choose an age-appropriate English book (but make sure the topic of the book is above reproach). Does he like to golf? Give him some golfing paraphernalia. Even if you are not well acquainted with your Chinese counterparts, bringing a gift from home, such as a bottle of wine from your home state, indicates an openness and thoughtfulness on your part that will win many hearts—and potentially business.

There are certain pitfall gifts to avoid. Do not give: cash, clocks (associated with death), knives (indicates "severing"), green hats (implies a wife/girlfriend has been unfaithful), or handkerchiefs (implies grief).

ENTERTAINMENT

There are multitudes of ways to keep yourself entertained in China. The favorite, of course, is karaoke. In the U.S., when there is karaoke at all, it is an afterthought. In China, it's the main event. One usually pays a small fee for the privilege of singing and customers vie for their turn. It's not necessary to have a good singing voice, just a willing spirit, if you want go on up and belt one out. All performers receive at least polite applause; many foreigners find that they receive an enthusiastic burst of clapping simply by virtue of being foreign, whether they sing like Frank Sinatra or like Roseanne. If you are being entertained for business in a karaoke bar, please make it a point to get up and sing if other members of your party do—to not participate can be seen as disinterested or churlish.

Other options for entertainment include nightclubs and discos, sports, and recreational activities such as Ping-Pong and tai chi. If you are living in an expatriate complex, it is likely that you will have some sort of recreational facilitates available.

China's traditional sports are *wǔshù*, a combined form of exercise and self-defense, *tàijíquán* or Chinese boxing, and *qìgōng*, a type of exercise which emphasizes controlling one's mind and regulating breathing for a longer, healthier life. Of the Western sports, soccer and baseball are the most popular, and both have professional leagues in China.

If you are looking for a little culture, your opportunities will be somewhat limited if you don't speak Chinese. Most foreign films are dubbed into Chinese. However, some of the upscale hotels show English language films. If you can locate Hong Kong movies, they usually have English subtitles.

China has enough scenery, historic places, art, architecture, and culture to keep a visitor busy for several years. You can, of course, take the do-it-yourself route, or you can look into the tours, classes, and so forth that are arranged within the expatriate community. If you travel around in China, you will have the chance to see regional and local activities, such as yak races in Tibet or Mongolian wrestling. And there are plenty of regional and local festivals and celebrations throughout the year.

HOMOSEXUALITY

China's official stance on homosexuality seems to be that it simply does not exist in China. It does, of course, but it is by and large not accepted by society. The Chinese "closet" is very, very deep and dark, and most Chinese gays won't be coming out any time soon. The threat of discrimination and even being fired from one's job looms large. Many gays and lesbians feel pressure to conform to society, to marry and have children. Many, in fact, are married and have children.

While homosexual relations are not illegal per se—that is, there is no actual law banning it—there is plenty of room within the system for harassment and even punishment. Laws that exist banning other forms of sexual interaction can be readily interpreted to include homosexual relations. The reality is that the authorities' attitude toward homosexuality is a mixture of the political and social climate, and of the person's own beliefs. Once in a while an event occurs that results in a "crackdown" on gays.

Harassment of gays is not uncommon, especially in those areas which are known to be frequented by gays. Discretion is essential; it is not recommended that gays discuss their sexuality or engage in public displays of affection (please note here that heterosexual public displays of affection are also not appropriate).

Having said that, there are both social and assistance networks for gays in China. There are plenty of gay bars, pubs, and hotels that operate without incident, largely due to keeping a low profile. The United Nations has provided funding for the distribution of condoms in China, and several semi-open gay bars and restaurants have opened in Beijing, Shanghai, and other major cities. One good source of information for locations and services on the Internet is www.utopia-asia.com.

FOOD

Chinese eat mostly at home, although increasing exposure to a Western lifestyle has been accompanied by an increase in eating out among the younger generation, especially in big cities such as Beijing, Shanghai, and Guangzhou. For the working class, a lunch box purchased from a favorite restaurant is a popular choice.

When Chinese do go to a restaurant, it is usually a family affair, with a half a dozen people or more crowded around the table. This, of course, provides a wonderful opportunity to try the many different dishes, which are placed in the middle of the table so the diners can help themselves. (A formal banquet is another matter altogether; please see the Business Step-by-Step section for more details on banquets.)

The cuisine of China is as diverse as its people. Generally speaking, the mainstay of the Chinese diet in the south is rice; in the north it is noodles. Spicy food tends to be popular in the west of China, particularly in the Hunan and Sichuan province.

Some ethnic specialties include the roast mutton kebab and crusty pancakes of Uygur, Kazakh, and Ozbek people; the stir-fried millet, fried sheep tail, and milk tea of Mongolians; Koreans' sticky rice cakes, cold noodles and kimchi (pickled vegetables); *zānbā* (roasted barley flour), and buttered tea, enjoyed by Tibetans; and the betel nuts chewed by Li, Jing, and Dai people.

HEALTH AND SAFETY

Healthcare in China is uneven at best. Competency and training of medical staff, available technology, and cleanliness of hospitals, clinics, and doctors' offices vary considerably. Many practitioners mix Western medicine with the more traditional idea of herbal remedies, acupuncture, etc. Given the rise in popularity of Eastern medical practices in the United States, this may not be unfamiliar to you.

Because of language issues (and a preference for Western medicine), most Americans seek out medical care from English-speaking doctors and dentists trained in Western medicine. There are a couple of ways to locate a doctor or dentist. You can inquire at your embassy or consulate, most of which keep a list of medical care facilities where your language is spoken. However, the best way to find a suitable physician or dentist is the same way you would do it at home: ask around for recommendations.

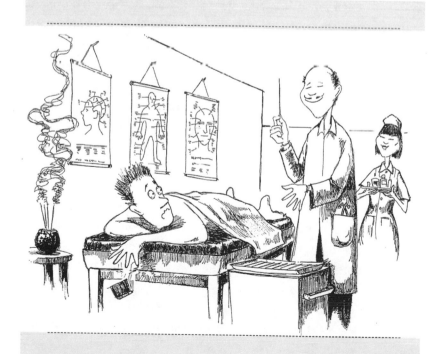

If you are staying at a hotel and become ill, there will probably be a nurse on staff. In the case of a more serious illness, a doctor can be called to come to your room if necessary.

While most minor ailments and injuries can be dealt with adequately in China, many expatriates choose to go elsewhere if they are in need of more advanced care, such as surgery or prenatal care. Both Hong Kong and Japan are nearby and have excellent, modern medical facilities. It is very important to arrange for your family's health insurance plans prior to arriving in China. You may need to get additional coverage, or even switch insurance companies, as it can be challenging to find insurance that is valid in China. Know in detail what benefits your insurance covers, including evacuation abroad for advanced care. In all cases you will have to pay out of pocket for medical care and apply for reimbursement against your insurance.

The most common ailments experienced by foreigners are upset stomachs (especially at first, while your system adjusts) and respiratory problems, such as asthma or allergic reactions due to pollution, dry, dusty air, and cigarette smoke. As mentioned earlier, tap water in China is not potable. Use a filtration system or bottled water. The health authorities recommend that you receive a battery of vaccinations before traveling to China. Contact the Center for Disease Control (see Appendix B) or your state health department for current information.

Although many remedies for common ailments are available in drugstores, it is wise to bring along a quantity of any prescription or non-prescription medicine or dietary supplements your family uses, including pain relievers and vitamins, especially for children. This is especially important for those susceptible to respiratory problems. Be sure to leave all drugs in their original bottles and make sure the labels are legible. In the case of prescription medication, ask your doctor to write a letter stating the generic name of the drug (brand names are not always the same around the world) and the reason you are taking the medication. While it may not be questioned, it is better to be prepared in case it does.

There is some concern about the issue of blood transfusions, especially the quality of the screening process. To complicate the matter, Chinese do not have Rh-negative blood, which can cause complications for those who have it. Ask your doctor about the advisability of banking your own blood for emergencies.

Here are some more tips and important pieces of information to ensure good health during your stay.

- The U.S. Public Health Services recommends certain medical precautions, such as immunizations, be taken before traveling to China, depending on your destination. You can contact them for specific information.
- Water in China is not potable; don't drink tap water. Your hotel room will be supplied with a carafe or thermos of filtered or bottled water, which you can easily get refilled by hotel staff. In restaurants, ask for an unopened bottle of water. In most better restaurants and hotels, ice is made from filtered water; however, it is best to avoid iced drinks in other places, as the ice was probably made from tap water. Better a warm drink than stomach problems!
- Air pollution in large cities in China is severe, especially in the winter. Many Chinese wear surgical masks to combat the problems. Pollution, the dry, dusty winter climate, and smoke may make wearing contact lenses difficult.
- The quality of medical care varies. Many doctors and nurses in China are qualified and competent. However, the medical technology lags behind the West and sanitary conditions are not as good as in the United States. As medical care is not free of charge, be sure you review your medical insurance to ensure that you will be covered during your stay in China. Find out in advance what procedures you will need to follow should you require medical attention.
- If you are staying in a hotel, you will usually have access to a doctor there. In Beijing there are two private clinics staffed by Western-qualified doctors; both are open twenty-four hours a day and have nurses and doctors who speak English.
- It's not uncommon to find Western medicine peacefully co-existing with traditional Chinese medicine in hospitals and doctors' offices. If you decide to seek out a doctor who practices Chinese medicine or acupuncture, use the same caution

you use in selecting your family doctor. Talk to the people you know for recommendations.

- Over-the-counter Western medicines (aspirin, cold medicine, vitamins, etc.) are available in drug stores and hotels. Chinese remedies for common ailments (stomachache, headache, etc.) are readily available.

- Chinese people have grown up surrounded by smokers; few realize that smoking is offensive to other people. Unless you are really allergic to cigarette smoke and truly can't bear it, you are advised to ignore the smoke or try to be diplomatic about it.

Water and Food Tips

Although tap water is treated with chlorine, it is not drinkable. Unless you want to boil all of your water, you can either install a water purification system or use bottled water, which is readily available. Be sure you fill your ice cube trays with purified water.

If you have children, you may be interested to know that water in China is not treated with fluoride, as American water is. You may want to speak to your dentist about any possible effects this may have and if an alternative fluoride treatment is necessary. You may also want to know that salt in China is generally not iodized, which has caused problems for China's children. If your family uses iodized salt, you may have to take a supply with you or look for it in the shops that serve foreigners.

Some areas of China use human excrement as fertilizer. It is advisable to wash fresh fruits and vegetables with a mild soap or a mild chlorine solution.

Canned goods packed in China are likely to contain some lead contamination, because lead is used to seal the can.

CRIME AND LEGAL ISSUES

China has a low rate of violent crime, and foreigners are generally not targeted. Nevertheless, take the same precautions as you would elsewhere to prevent pickpocketing and theft of your belongings, as it will be evident that you are a tourist.

Remember that while you are in China, you are subject to the local laws and regulations. These can be significantly different than those at home, and the Chinese legal system does not afford individuals the same protection as the U.S. legal system. Penalties for breaking the law can be more severe than in the United States, and offenders, knowingly or not, can end up in jail or deported.

As mentioned earlier, literature and photographs that may seem harmless to you may be deemed pornographic or political in nature, and can be seized, as can documents judged to be intended for religious proselytizing. The latter, religious proselytizing, even passing out material of a religious nature, is forbidden, and if you are found to be carrying more than is appropriate for your personal use, you can be fined and/or detained.

Emergency Numbers

Although some emergency telephone numbers differ throughout China, the following are valid for Beijing, Shanghai, and Guangzhou. You can check the local yellow pages for the valid telephone numbers in other areas

> **Police:** 110 (throughout China)
> **Fire:** 119
> **Ambulance/Medical emergency:** 120

POST OFFICE

Surface, air, and express services are available in China. Carrier companies, such as FedEx, UPS, and DHL, are available, but operate only in large cities. Remember that the order of a Chinese address is opposite that of a typical U.S. address. If you are sending mail outside of China, it can help expedite delivery if you put the destination country in Chinese characters as well as Roman characters.

Post offices can usually be found at airports, on main streets, and near tourist attractions. International mail may need to be sent from a specific post office, such as the International Post Office in Beijing. If you are sending a parcel from China, leave the package unopened until it is inspected at the post office. Take your supplies with you, or purchase them at the post office, and pack up your box after the inspection.

The Chinese postal service can be a trying experience. Expect to wait in line or be sent to yet another line and don't expect a smile from the postal employee. You can avoid some of the hassle by using the postal service that is available in some large hotels in major cities. Unfortunately, these services do not include international parcel shipment, but you can buy postage stamps and take care of some other tasks there. Express or insured mail must go through the post office.

If friends and relatives will be shipping you packages from home, be sure to inform them of China's restrictions on items that cannot be brought into the country. Spot checks are made and the inclusion of pornography (remember that standards are different in China; something you might consider mainstream may be deemed pornographic) or politically sensitive material will result in the entire package being confiscated. If a parcel arrives for you, you will receive a slip of paper from the post office (written in Chinese only). Take the slip of paper and your passport to the designated location to retrieve your package. If your package didn't arrive, it may have been confiscated by customs.

TIPPING

Tipping is not very common in China, although it is standard for some services in major hotels, such as the bellhop. Like gift giving, tipping involves a small ritual of reluctance to accept the tip and insistence on the part of the tipper. If you would like to tip a hotel maid, tour guide or other service providers, you can give him or her American cigarettes, books, or other inexpensive items instead of money. One does not tip in restaurants. You will find, though, that most of better restaurants add a 10%–15% service charge onto your bill.

SIX

BUSINESS ENVIRONMENT

Recent events in China have led to the evolution of the business environment. The privatization of some state-owned companies and the growth of the private sector have brought with them many changes. The Chinese business environment today is in a state of flux as the Chinese move from a planned economy to a market-driven economy. On the level of company structure and environment, there are very distinct differences between state-owned companies and private ones, with the recently privatized companies falling somewhere in between.

State-owned companies have a history of obligation to ensure the livelihood of their employees, providing lifetime employment and caring for employees even into their retirement years. Many continue to operate at a loss as a result of this legacy. Up until recently the responsibility of management was to produce whatever was required by the current five-year plan established by the government, regardless of cost or quality. In recent years, however, state-owned companies have been charged with fiscal responsibility. The government now allows poorly-run state companies to lay off employees (retraining program are provided for laid-off employees), to cut salaries, and even to declare bankruptcy. Every sector of business in China has become more profit driven. The government continues to implement programs to promote growth in all industries, providing protection especially for nascent industries such as the automobile industry.

State-owned companies, whose employees traditionally had guaranteed salaries regardless of their performance, tended to breed a lack of initiative and low standards. New economic incentives and performance measurements with organizations have made employees increasingly aware of their responsibility. Change, however, comes slowly, and many state-owned companies are still struggling with the burden of instilling in their employees new ways of thinking and working. The initial growing pains have been evident. Employees in management positions, no longer guaranteed their jobs but still in a position where their performance evaluation is largely determined by personal connections rather than ability and accomplishment, have tended to look after their own self-interest and have focused on short-term results. Continued restructuring and the influence of Western-style management have helped achieve a balance between profit-driven growth and social responsibility. As a result, holdovers from the days of old-style state-run companies have slowly begun to disappear.

In the private sector, where the primary goal has always been profit, a very different environment exists. The traditional role of employer as provider was mitigated by the responsibility of the employee to contribute toward favorable results. Salaries were higher, but lifetime employment was not part of the package. Thus the private sector has had an easier time adapting to the demands of a market economy. Don't, however, make the mistake of thinking that because China has adopted a market economy Chinese organizations operate the same way Western, especially American, organizations do. Chinese business continues to reflect, to varying degrees, China's unique cultural history of conformity, personal connections, and placing the group before the individual.

GOVERNMENT AND BUSINESS

Government and business are inextricably intertwined in China. It was only a handful of years ago that the Chinese government began its privatization program. This was not a sweeping reform; plenty of state-owned enterprises still exist. And while the government touts its recent shift from a planned economy to a market-driven one, it nevertheless keeps its fingers in the economic pie, subsidizing technology, providing credit to export industries, protecting developing industries with lowered tariffs, and so on.

Another way in which the Chinese government continues to manage industry is through import, export, and investment quotas. Once the established quotas have been met, the doors are closed until next year's quotas are set. Since one must be authorized to import or export, it is helpful if one establishes and maintains key contacts within the government.

These recent reforms have resulted in a change in the way that China does business. In the old state-owned enterprises, the government absorbed both the profits and the losses of its various businesses. This, of course, meant that there was very little incentive for good management, as the result was the same, no matter what one did. The newly-privatized business, of course, must be operated at a profit, as many of the new businesses are being started by Chinese entrepreneurs. Even the managers of business that continue to be state run now have greater control over the operations of their companies and have responsibility for losses and profits. The new incentives for good management, efficiency, and quality are clear.

The Chinese business environment can be extremely confusing and exasperating, in part because the government tends to change the policies and rules for doing business without warning. It is especially difficult for foreigners, because the government is disinclined to discuss new business policies with foreigners. It is therefore in your best interest to find a local Chinese partner or consultant who can keep you abreast of any changes. These people can also be invaluable contacts with the government, a favorable situation which will in turn grease the wheels for your company to receive the necessary government approvals.

THE CHAIN OF COMMAND

State-owned or private, Chinese companies have a distinctly hierarchical structure. Decisions are made only with the approval of upper management, especially in state-owned companies and governmental agencies.

The highest ranking person in a Chinese company is the general manager (*zŏng jīnglǐ*). Until the early 1980s, the local Communist Party Secretary had veto power on all major decisions made within a company. Now, in theory at least, the general manager is the sole leader of the organization. The reality of any organization, however, depends largely on the general political climate and the individual personalities of the general manager and party secretary. Party secretaries with important connections within the government can have considerable influence on the operation of the company. It is important not to overlook the power of either of these players. Despite appearing relatively innocuous, a person with ties to the government can wield enormous informal authority.

On paper the general manager is elected by the company's Workers' Representative Congress. Here, too, the reality is quite different, and most general managers have complete discretion over the selection of managerial candidates who are then rubber stamped by the Congress.

The upper echelons of Chinese management are the *cadres*

(*ganbu*), who hold the most senior level management positions. These *cadres* are appointed by the general manager. They, in turn, control the selection of senior- and mid-level managers. Again, those individuals with party support are the most influential.

The real power of the organization lies with the few individuals at the top of the corporate totem pole. Middle management in most companies is neither equipped nor inclined to make decisions. Rather, mid-level managers wait for the decisions of their superiors, which they then carry out.

In theory, the workers have some leverage via the Workers' Congress that exists in every organization, in system instituted in the 1950. On paper the Congress' duty is to review managerial decisions, to be involved in decision making, and to offer suggestions through its representatives. In reality, however, the Congress is usually limited to decisions that involve working conditions, but not the overall management or strategy of the organization.

THE WORK UNIT (DĀNWÈI)

Once upon a time, each individual was assigned to a *dānwèi* upon graduation from university. The *dānwèi* could be a factory, office, farm, school, etc. The *dānwèi* system guaranteed lifetime employment, but, unfortunately for the worker, the assignments were made by government agencies where decisions were rarely based on the individual's goals or talents.

Although *dānwèi* is translated as "work unit," its actual description goes much deeper. The nature of the *dānwèi* is more like an extended family in that in addition to a job, the employee receives a host of benefits, including housing, childcare, health insurance, and pensions. Some *dānwèi* even provide extended facilities and social subsidies, such as a cafeteria where workers and their families can eat at little or no cost. The *dānwèi*, in turn, controls the career of its employees. Each individual has a personnel file which records his or her family background, job performance, and other activities; it is virtually impossible for the employee to transfer to another *dānwèi* without this file, and therefore without your current *dānwèi*'s permission. The *dānwèi* reflects in many ways the Confucian beliefs, with the company acting as provider and protector, the parental role, in exchange for absolute loyalty, the role of the child, in this case the employee.

The *dānwèi* has been called the "Iron Rice Bowl", symbolizing lifetime employment and social support. Under this system, university graduates are guaranteed jobs, although by no means jobs that match either their qualifications or interests.

The government has recently begun to dismantle the *dānwèi* system, although there are certainly those who would prefer to retain this traditional system, both for its security and for its social structure. Outside of the *dānwèi*, university graduates in particular have a chance to choose a job more compatible with their abilities at a considerably higher salary and with greater job mobility. The trade-off, of course, is that job security is relinquished and the many social services traditionally taken care of by the employer become the responsibility of the employee.

BUSINESS HOURS

Despite the fact that it extends across six time zones, all of China keeps one standard time. Therefore, business hours vary somewhat throughout China, beginning anywhere from 8:00 A.M. to 9:30 A.M. and ending between 5:00 A.M. and 7:30 P.M., with a one to three hour lunch break at midday. Shops set their own hours. The typical civil servant works from 8:00 A.M. to 5:00 P.M., with a lunch break from noon to 1:30 P.M. Employees, especially in government offices, leave as early as 3:00 P.M. during the summer. There is some seasonal variation in this schedule, as lunch breaks and quitting times are extended to take advantage of the longer days.

Daylight Saving Time begins on the second Sunday in April and ends on the second Sunday in September.

OFFICE SPACE

The layout of offices in China varies depending on the type of organization. In state-owned companies or governmental agencies, rooms containing three to five desks are common. Japanese-owned companies often prefer the Japanese arrangement of having an open area where most of the department staff works together at tables or desks. For companies with Western investment, Western-style cubicles are typical. Higher level personnel receive separate offices in all cases.

Status in the office is indicated by the assignment of a separate office, the location of the office, and even the comparable luxury of office furniture. Personal secretaries are not found except at the highest levels. A secretarial/typing pool is available to those at lower levels.

Chinese are not inclined to place personal items, such as family photos, on their desks or in their offices. Many Chinese do, however, place a plant in their work area. The type of plant is usually selected for its ability to bring fortune.

The quality and availability of equipment varies. Even in Western joint ventures, it is not likely that every individual will have a computer on his or her desk. All e-mail may go to a central computer, where it is printed out for the recipient. The telephone systems generally do not have the latest technology, such as individual voice mailboxes. These factors can cause quite a challenge for communication with a Chinese company.

WOMEN IN BUSINESS

The traditional role of women in China was that of accessories to men, not their equals. Men were historically able to have multiple wives and concubines. They had the right to divorce their wives for not bearing a son, for being jealous, and other reasons. Women, meanwhile, could not divorce their husbands for any reason.

In the 1950s women began appearing in civil service and business positions thanks to the reforms following the founding of the People's Republic of China. Today in urban areas it is becoming more and more common to see women in business and government, although few have reached the higher levels of management. In rural areas, however, many women continue to solely fill the traditional roles of wife and mother.

Despite technical equality in modern China, women still face some difficulty in the workplace. The weights of the balance remain tipped in favor of men for various reasons, not the least of which is the fact that women require maternity leave, making them less desirable employees in certain positions. The few women who have risen to management positions can find themselves faced with resistance from their more traditional colleagues.

Tips for Women in Business

As a foreign business woman, it is important to understand that you are not subject to the same standards as Chinese women in business. In fact, you will probably find that most Chinese, men and women alike, hold great respect for you, believing that your company has great faith in you to have chosen you for the assignment. This is contingent, of course, on their recognizing your position in the company. The worst thing a foreign woman can do is to allow the initial impression that she is of no consequence. Women who do not correct such assumptions immediately will not have an easy time of accomplishing their goals.

There are many things a woman can do to ensure that she gains the respect of her Chinese counterparts. A letter stating her leadership position, qualifications, and accomplishments should be sent by the company before the woman's arrival.

If a woman is leading a delegation, her company should provide a list of delegates, again clearly indicating that she is heading the party. In addition, the title on her business card should reflect a position of authority. She should be the first person introduced to the Chinese senior management; she can then introduce her subordinates.

If a woman is the leader of a negotiation or meeting, all interaction should essentially funnel through her. She should be the first person to respond to inquiries. Questions can then be delegated to an appropriate team member. A woman's subordinates should not question or contradict her in public.

Businesswomen will be included in business dinners and entertainment. You should try to accept; if you cannot accept, officially designate someone as her representative.

A woman's success in China depends on her team members, as well as her own actions. It is essential that everyone on the team be thoroughly prepared before landing in China. Team members should be prepared to demonstrate that the power rests with their leader.

Negative comments or criticism of the issue of women's rights in China, especially in a business environment, should be avoided. You must remember, after all, that you are a visitor to the country, and you may not have a complete understanding of the situation. One good example is China's policy of allowing families only one child. While many foreigners see this as an invasion of one's privacy and personal decision-making, Chinese do not necessarily think the same way. You may be surprised to find that most Chinese women realize that China has a serious population problem and agree with the policy. With over 6 billion people on the planet today, this policy may have merits you haven't considered.

SEVEN

BUSINESS STEP-BY-STEP

If you wish to succeed,
consult three old people.

—Chinese proverb

The key to doing business successfully with Chinese is to immediately throw out your assumptions about how business should be done. Taking the time to learn not only the dos and don'ts of Chinese business protocol, but understanding the way that Chinese do business will go a long way toward your success in China. In this section we'll look at some general concepts as well as specific types of protocol that should be kept in mind when doing business in China.

MAKING CONTACT

If you are looking to begin doing business in or with China, you can make contact in a variety of ways. The most successful ventures, however, begin with a third party introduction. Intermediary introductions are especially helpful for large or complicated projects or if you need to make contact with high-ranking government officials or state-owned companies. An introduction can open doors that would otherwise stay shut, help you find the real decision-maker and change a "No" to a "Yes."

Begin with any personal contacts you might already have. Do you have an employee, supplier, service provider, or client, Chinese or otherwise, who has established relationships in China? As you search for links to China, don't limit yourself to your own company or industry. Because networking is such an integral part of doing business in China, you may find an indirect route to the perfect contact. For example, your lawyer, who was involved in negotiating a joint venture contract in China, may have a government contact. Don't hesitate to take advantage of contacts, even indirect ones, or to refer to them as an entrance to doing business in China.

If you or your company does not currently have any contacts in China, there are still ways to make contact through opportunities such as trade fairs or official trade missions. There are several ways to initiate contact, including the Chinese Ministry of Foreign Relations and Trade, embassies or consulates both in China and in the United States, the U.S. Department of Commerce, trade councils, and international chambers of commerce. Additionally, there are more than 40,000 Chinese students and scholars in American universities and colleges. They usually have good contacts and connections at home. They may be able to introduce you to the right people if you establish a connection before you leave.

Before agreeing to do business with any company in China, be sure to do your homework and research both the company and the industry thoroughly and continue to monitor them. Most industries are strictly regulated by the government and the rules and regulations can change without warning. If the project involves importing or exporting, verify that the company has received governmental permission to import or export the product in question. Verify also the company's ability to pay for any products and services you will be supplying.

The amount of energy and time you will have to put into establishing an appropriate contact in China can vary depending on the type of organization you are trying to reach. It is relatively easier to make contact with smaller private businesses than with state-owned businesses. The goal is to gain direct access to the person in charge, preferably in person. However, be aware that establishing contact and reaching a business agreement can take a considerable amount of time.

If possible, have your mutual contact make the introduction, by letter or fax if necessary. You can then establish contact with a fax, followed by a telephone call. Be sure that you state your reason for contact when you initially approach the Chinese organization. Emphasize the benefits to Chinese, including not only profit or capital, but also technology and favorable treatment from the Chinese government. And don't forget to drop the name of the person who referred you or any mutual acquaintances you might have. Be prepared to be persistent, following up consistently.

Unless you are part of a large internationally-known organization, you will have to first establish your credibility with the Chinese organization. The easiest way to do this is through a reputable intermediary. However, if you are going it alone, you will need to provide the Chinese company or agency that will be sponsoring you with essential background information about your own company. Because business travel to China requires a sponsor, who becomes fully responsible for you, the guest, you may have to invest considerable time in convincing the Chinese organization that it is to its benefit to arrange a face-to-face meeting to discuss your business.

Establishing a business relationship with a Chinese company or agency can take months or even years. Before you decide to make contact, you must be willing to make a long-term commitment to China.

GENERAL BUSINESS ETIQUETTE

Before we go any further, let's take a look at some important points concerning general business etiquette in China.

Chinese greetings are usually quite formal, especially in business. Do not expect a smile when you meet people. Although a bow or nod is the traditional greeting in China, many Chinese who have had experience with Westerners, especially in business, expect to use a handshake. Wait for your Chinese colleague to offer his hand first. If you do bow, keep your hands at your side and out of your pockets.

After the bow or handshake, business cards (called *míng piàn* in Chinese—"name cards") should be exchanged. Use both hands to both present your card and receive others' cards.

You should have had your own card translated into Mandarin Chinese on one side for the benefit of Chinese. If you want to have a "Chinese" name, seek assistance from a Chinese person; if you merely translate the syllables of your name, you may end up with a name that has unpleasant connotations. Gold is a prestigious color to have on your business card. On your card, omit middle initials in your name. You can add a courtesy title (Mr., Mrs., or Miss) to aid your Chinese colleagues.

When you receive a business card, take a moment to examine it and be sure you understand the other person's name and rank. Don't write on someone's card in his or her presence. Even more importantly, men shouldn't stow their Chinese colleague's business card in your wallet—think about which part of your anatomy your wallet will end up next to. Use a business card holder that is kept in your breast pocket or briefcase. If you are sitting down following the business card exchange, you can set the cards before you on the table to refer to them.

Chinese typically begin all conversations, including business ones, with some small talk. This may be about your trip or accommodations if you are a business traveller meeting your colleagues for the first time. However, even on subsequent visits, small talk is necessary. This period of small talk can be a gold mine for you, since you can take the opportunity to find out more about the person. Knowing about a person's interests and family can help you pick out a suitable gift in the future; since gift giving is an essential part of the Chinese culture, this information can come in quite handy. You can ask about your colleagues' children (age, school, interests, etc.), spouse, or parents. Other good topics of conversation include your respective hometowns, educational background (school attended, major, etc.), hobbies, travels, and so on.

Direct eye contact is considered rude by many Chinese, especially when addressing a superior. Don't be surprised if someone seems to be avoiding your gaze; it's a gesture of respect. If you are meeting a group, address the most senior person first. The group will probably line up in order of seniority to be greeted. If you came with other people, be sure the senior members of both parties are introduced first, followed by the others in descending order of importance.

Be punctual for business meetings. An early arrival shows respect; a late arrival indicates disrespect for your host(s). Tea is usually served at meetings; don't refuse your host's hospitality. Just as it is common to have a brief period of social talk about the weather, the flight, etc., you should also be prepared to give a brief presentation on your company, if it's your first visit, and hear about your counterparts' company. But be careful with your presentation material, since some colors have specific connotations. See the section on Gifts for more on this.

BUSINESS COMMUNICATION

Telephone

Next to a personal appointment, the telephone is the most effective way to elicit a response in China. Just getting the right person on the phone can be difficult, though. Most offices do not have voice mail, and messages left with a coworker are not especially effective, particularly in a state-owned business. Your goal must be a direct conversation with the appropriate person. You cannot expect that a detailed message left with a colleague will have any impact; it may not even reach the person. Exercise both patience and persistence. It may take several tries to reach the right person or to have him or her return your call. Once you have reached the person, check back in every few days to make sure everything is going in the right direction. Frequent communication facilitates success.

E-mail

While you can use e-mail to supplement your business communications, it is not advisable to rely on it as a primary means of communication. Internet access is more expensive in China, and most Chinese companies do not provide computers to every employee. Although you may be accustomed to checking your e-mail every hour, Chinese are not. They may pick up their messages every couple of days. In general, the Internet is used more as a tool for information research than as a method of communication.

When using e-mail, be sure you clearly indicate the intended recipient in the body of the message. This is especially important if there is one central e-mail address for the whole company. Putting the name and title of the recipient in the message will ensure that it reaches the proper person.

GETTING TO THE TOP

Making your way into the inner sanctum of the top-most management in any organization can be a difficult endeavor. The structure of the typical Chinese organization is very hierarchical, and decisions come from the top and move down. If you present your idea or proposal to a junior staff member, chances are pretty good that nothing will happen because that person does not have decision-making authority. Even if a junior staff member does recommend your proposal for consideration, it can take a long time to filter up to the highest level of the company.

As usual, personal relationships play a major part in decision making. It therefore behooves you to work your way into a personal relationship with someone high on the food chain who can act as a liaison with the company's general manager. A personal introduction to someone with the general manager's ear, such as his assistant, secretary, or direct subordinate, is ideal. If you have a direct route to the decision maker, you can expedite the process by receiving informal approval from him. In the case that your proposal is rejected, also informally, you can go back to your drawing board without wasting time waiting for the necessary approval.

If you are unable to establish a personal relationship with upper management, you will need to present your business proposal to successive layers of management until you reach a decision maker. Individual employees, especially those at the lower level, have little power to make decisions, but they can offer a recommendation of your proposal to their immediate supervisor. Even in this situation, having a positive relationship with the person to whom you present your idea can help get his support for the proposal.

THE FIRST MEETING

The initial meeting, and sometimes one or two subsequent meetings, is generally an opportunity for the visiting company and the sponsor company to get to know each other. Unfortunately, some Americans interpret this relationship-building period as a lack of genuine interest, and give up after the first visit. On the contrary, as China's culture prizes relationships, this first meeting is crucial to your overall deal.

During your visit, your Chinese hosts will invariably invite you to at least one banquet. You should reciprocate by also hosting a banquet, perhaps on the last day of meetings. Hosting is done at restaurants, clubs, hotels, or entertainment centers; choose a first-class location if possible. If you need assistance arranging the dinner, your hosts can help you select an appropriate restaurant.

MEETING PROTOCOL

Chinese meetings are more formal than most American meetings, whether you are negotiating a major contract or simply calling on Chinese business partners. Every member of your team should dress and comport themselves in an appropriately businesslike fashion.

Any visit to China is a potential occasion to meet with senior business or government members. Even if you will be conducting the particulars of business with people on a lower level, these meetings, no matter how brief or symbolic, show goodwill and sincere interest in doing business with the Chinese company. Cancellations and delays are always a possibility when the upper echelons are involved. Should this happen to you, be sure to express understanding, not dissatisfaction. It's likely that your Chinese hosts will try to find a way to make it up to you with a special event or dinner.

Proper protocol is important at all meetings. Your host will be in the meeting room to greet you. Your team should allow the leader to enter first followed in descending order of rank. The most senior person on the Chinese team will be introduced by a junior member; he will then introduce his team. Then it is time for the senior member of the visiting team to introduce his or her team members. If you are meeting for the first time, business cards will be exchanged, as described earlier in this chapter. Most Chinese are familiar with the Western handshake, but it is often accompanied by a polite nod. You can follow suit.

After the introductions are complete, your team will be directed to the appropriate side of the table. The senior person of each team sits in the middle of his team. Your team leader should be given the courtesy of sitting before the other team members. The meeting begins with small talk. Be prepared to chat about your flight, your accommodations, the weather and other innocuous topics. Following the small talk, the Chinese leader will make a few welcoming comments. When the time comes for your presentation, be sure to begin with the basics, including some background about your company. When was your company founded? Where is it located? How many employees does it have? And, of course, what is the full line of products or services that it offers? Chinese prefer to see the "big picture" before getting down to specifics.

Meetings are concluded as formally as they are begun. A closing statement from your host will hopefully indicate their intention to form a close partnership with your company. The visiting team's leader should then express appreciation and also express a desire for a long-term relationship. These closing statements can be very important. The Chinese leader's statements can give you clues (albeit often hidden ones) about their interest, or lack of it, in your company. By the same token, if the visiting leader fails to mention future relations, it may be interpreted by Chinese as a lack of interest. A round of handshakes follows, beginning with the most senior members, then your team will be escorted to the door or elevator.

Come prepared for the meetings. Although the hotel may offer a business center, it's usually better to bring sufficient copies of your documents with you. If you have any special requests to make of your hosts for the meeting, such as presentation equipment, make them as early as possible. Don't assume the request can be met unless you specifically have confirmation. A lack of an answer can usually be interpreted as a negative. The Chinese company is not likely to have sophisticated presentation equipment available, so it is better to bring your own—don't forget any necessary voltage transformers and plug adapters. It's never a bad idea to bring low-tech backup presentation material, such as handouts or flipchart pages, just in case. Typing up and distributing notes from the meeting can also help ensure clear communication between your companies.

Any series of meetings with Chinese call for at least two dinners. The first one, usually on the first or second day, will be scheduled by your Chinese hosts. It is up to you as the visitor to schedule a similar event on the evening of one of the final meeting day. This should be an elaborate affair, and everyone on your team should attend. Help in planning and scheduling the event is as close as your hotel staff or a nice nearby restaurant. Quite often either one can handle

all of the details; you need only describe the nature of the event and the number of guests.

NEGOTIATING THE DEAL

It is important to select the right representatives to send to meet with Chinese. It is appropriate to send at least one high-ranking member of your organization as a sign of your commitment to the project. The Chinese organization will select a team that closely matches yours in terms of rank of the individual members. Note that the high-ranking Chinese individuals who welcome you and who attend the ceremonial functions of your negotiations, such as the president or general manager, will probably not be directly involved in the negotiation itself; however, they are the real decision makers in the organization, so their support is crucial.

It will probably be on your second or third trip to China that the real business negotiation gets started. Again, it is critical that you carefully select the members of your negotiating team. It is essential to have at least one person who is able to answer any and all technical questions relating to your product and service. Most teams sent to negotiate also include at least one person who is in a position to make decisions on behalf of the organization. It is highly advisable to also include on your team someone who can act as an interpreter and cultural guide. Refer to our section on interpreters at the end of this chapter.

If you opt to use a trade specialist or consulting firm to act as an intermediary for your negotiation, you must also take care to develop and nurture your own personal relationships with your Chinese partners.

The Chinese team will be made up of specialists from various divisions and one leader who will act as spokesperson. Developing a close and personal connection with the leader of the negotiating team and with any high-ranking individuals you meet is key to a successful negotiation. Especially if you are negotiating with a government-run organization, you may also notice a shadow observer to the negotiation, a person who may not be introduced. This is in all likelihood the party secretary. Almost all contracts between foreign and Chinese companies must be approved by the government; do not underestimate the influence of political representatives.

Provide as much information as possible well before the meeting. There are several reasons for this. For one thing, it will help ensure that the Chinese organization includes the appropriate personnel in meetings. If there is any uncertainty at all about the purpose of the meeting, you may find yourself meeting not with the necessary people, but instead with a type of liaison officer who has been sent only to elicit information about your intentions and who is not in a position to make decisions of any type.

The more information you are able to send in advance, the better prepared the Chinese team will be. Unlike the typical American team, which sends a decision maker to lead the negotiating, Chinese usually send a team whose goal is to gather information which will then be taken back to the decision makers for consideration. If you have not sent any information that the Chinese team can digest before meeting with you, you will have to spend more time waiting for them to relay information to the decision makers and for them to receive instructions from above.

Whenever possible, try to elicit input from your Chinese counterparts in the pre-negotiation stages. An exchange of views will help you scout out any concerns or problems on the Chinese side, allowing you to address those issues during the negotiation.

Sending an exact list of who will be attending the negotiation, their functions, and their expected contribution to the meetings, and extracting a similar list from the Chinese side, will also help streamline the process to a degree.

The negotiation itself can be divided into two stages: technical and administrative. The technical stage is where all of the technical requirements are discussed in detail, questions about the product or service are asked and answered. This stage can be quite lengthy and is guaranteed to test the patience of the American team members if they are expecting a quick resolution.

The second stage is to hammer out the details of the transaction itself. It's likely that the Chinese side will have essentially two teams, one to handle each aspect of the negotiation. Be sure that your team includes individuals who are capable of fulfilling all of your needs. At least one person should be available to answer any technical questions, if applicable, and one team member must be able to negotiate on behalf of your company.

The pace of the negotiation itself will be different than it is in the United States. Rather than being a series of questions and answers, it more resembles an alternating series of mini-presentations from both sides. This is aided by the fact that both parties have distributed information to each other in the pre-negotiation stages.

As the guest, you will probably be expected to have the floor first. It's appropriate to begin with a brief presentation about your company's background. Don't expect an immediate response to any part of your presentation. Your Chinese colleagues will probably not have the authority to respond directly, and even if one does, it is generally preferred that all issues be taken back for private discussion within the group so a group consensus can be reached.

The team leaders direct the flow of the negotiation. The other members of the team are expected to show respect to the rank and status of the leader, providing input when asked but doing nothing to contradict the leader or otherwise cause him to lose face. It's considered rude to interrupt another person while he or she is talking. However, your Chinese colleagues may respond to your comments with occasional nods or grunts. Do not make the mistake of taking these as indications of agreement. They are more accurately translated as "I heard you" or "I understand you" than as "I agree with you."

One key point to keep in mind is that you should never put any one person on the spot. Questions and requests should be phrased in such a way as to allow the other person to maintain face, especially if the information requested is not immediately available. For example, saying "We would like to receive such-and-such information" is preferable to a more direct demand. Of course, the requested information may take some time for you to receive if the answer isn't within the scope of those present, or if the Chinese team feels it needs permission from a superior to provide that information.

NEGOTIATING TACTICS

Generally speaking, the American negotiating style is a series of offers and counteroffers until an agreement is reached that will result in a win-win situation. Both sides sit down at the table knowing just how much flexibility they have in terms of price, time and other factors. They begin at the upper limits and allow themselves to be negotiated down from there.

The Chinese style is quite different. As mentioned above, it is doubtful that any of the Chinese team members will be decision-makers. Their negotiating position will have been discussed by the powers that be beforehand and will have been set for them. Chinese do not like surprises. Therefore, if you spring new information, a different price, or ask for information from them, they will probably need to take this information back to their superiors for discussion. Your team, on the other hand, is expected to be able to make decisions quickly. Chinese are out to win, although the final result obviously has to be one that both parties can live with.

Americans negotiating with Chinese for the first time often feel that they are being pumped for information. Chinese delegation may even rotate its members throughout the course of the negotiating, with each new person asking the same questions as the last. Indeed, it is not unusual for a Chinese company to use the meetings with your team for its own benefit, such as gathering technical information that it can use for its own purposes. Therefore it is important that each member of your team understand just how much information—especially proprietary or sensitive information—you are willing or able to share with your Chinese counterparts.

One of the most effective techniques that Chinese use over and over again when negotiating with Americans is simple patience. Westerners in general and Americans in particular are notorious for their impatience. Chinese therefore simply use a take-it-slowly approach, which prompts their American counterparts into revealing more or making other concessions when Chinese do not respond immediately.

Another facet of this ploy is time. The above-mentioned take-it-slowly approach can be used to drag the negotiations out until the American side changes its position to one more favorable to the Chinese side in light of a fast-approaching deadline or termination of the business trip.

The only effective defenses against this delaying tactic are patience and having alternatives. If your team is part of a larger organization, you must have the support of upper management, including a reasonable or flexible deadline. You should build enough padding into your timeline to include multiple trips to China, the necessary time to build a relationship, and the inevitable delays. If you have leveraged your options by meeting with several different organizations, you will be in a better position to walk out of a negotiation that is going nowhere—just be sure before you do that you have thoroughly evaluated the situation and that you have not mistaken a genuine need to work things through for a stalling tactic.

Despite the general Chinese propensity for maintaining a calm demeanor, tempers sometimes flare during negotiations. In fact, some Chinese use anger as part of their negotiating repertoire. This is often just a show of anger, designed to intimidate the opponent. This tactic is reserved to senior members of the team; junior members of the Chinese team will not express anger openly in front of their superior.

A few tactics that may enter the negotiation may be unfamiliar to you. Personal obligations play a very important part in Chinese business, and indeed life in general. The strings of personal obligation can even be tugged on the foreigner. Chinese may also expect concessions from you stemming from the fact that you belong to a rich American organization and they are poor Chinese, new to the game. It is not uncommon for Chinese negotiation tactics to include an element of shaming you into giving more to help a country struggling to catch up.

And finally, although Chinese generally favor an indirect communication style, the negotiating table allows for more latitude for bluntness, especially when the other party represents a foreign company.

CLOSING THE DEAL

In general, negotiating with Chinese may seem to progress in fits and starts. Your initial meeting might be followed by the beginning of a serious negotiation, then a period of seeming inactivity while Chinese deliberate, followed by more meetings. Even when an agreement is reached, you will probably have to spend a significant amount of time on the actual contract.

Don't make the assumption that your idea of a contract meshes with theirs. To Americans, the contract is a map of the path of the partnership, where the legal rights and responsibilities of both parties are set out in detail. To Chinese, the contract outlines a general understanding; the details can be filled in later and are flexible as necessary depending on new laws, rules, or regulations and the needs of both parties.

Although there is a possibility of arbitration in contract disputes, remember that in China, as one international lawyer explains, the laws are generally negotiable and in most instances tend to favor the Chinese party. Your continued good relationship with Chinese will be more valuable to the fulfillment of contractual obligations than the contract.

Once you have signed the contract with your Chinese partner, festivities are in order. Your new partners will host a banquet and you will be expected to host one. It would be even more impressive to fly in a senior member of your company to host the celebration and signing ceremony. Most good restaurants provide banquet facilities and can even be relied on to take care of all of the details of the banquet, ensuring that the appropriate dishes are served, seating is properly arranged and so on. It is especially important at this more formal event that the proper protocol be closely observed. Consult with your cultural guide, if you have one, or a junior member of the

Chinese team about any details you are unsure of, such as who should be on the guest list, how to issue invitations, and the relative ranking of each member of the Chinese team.

The successful conclusion of a deal is also the time to exchange gifts. Each member of the Chinese team should be presented with a gift appropriate to his rank and contribution to the negotiation. Suitable gifts might include calculators, watches (NOT clocks), or leather day planners. For more gift-giving ideas—including gift taboos—refer to the "Gift" section on page 149.

By the Way...

CHOP, CHOP!

Name chops have made their mark in China throughout dozens of centuries, dating back to a time when much of the population was illiterate. One therefore signed one's name with a seal, or name chop (yìn zhāng.) The tradition has carried into today's world, where it can be difficult, if not impossible, to complete a legal contract without the imprint of the chop. Chops use a special red ink, called dragon's blood. If you will be in China for an extended period, or if you'll be doing business there on a regular basis, consider getting yourself a name chop.

PRESENTING YOUR IDEAS AND MAKING SPEECHES

When you are presenting your business proposal to your Chinese counterparts, it is important to connect your interests to theirs. Don't rely on the prospect of profits to sell your idea. Emphasize also the benefits your company brings to the table. Important concerns for Chinese are capital investment, receiving new technology, job creation, and higher salaries. The Chinese company needs to see that it, too, will benefit from any partnership, that the sole purpose of the venture is not to put money in already-rich Western pockets. Just as they would anywhere, charts, figures, and diagrams will help make the presentation clearer.

Prepare yourself by researching the relevant Chinese regulations and policies. The government has adopted several preferential policies to entice foreign investment that can benefit both you and your Chinese partner.

If you are making a more formal presentation, you will have to throw out your American "guide to great presentations" book, which probably advises you to break the ice with humor and stick to the bottom line. When you present to a Chinese audience, remember that not only do Chinese not start their presentations with a joke, humor simply does not translate. It is much better to begin with a statement that states your appreciation for the opportunity to present your idea and mention your company's wish for a long and fruitful partnership with their Chinese partners.

If you are presenting to high officials, it's best to keep it short; these presentations are more about form than substance. However, when you are presenting your idea to a team led by middle management, you will want to make sure you cover the topic thoroughly. These types of meetings also begin with statements of goodwill, and should be followed by an introduction to your company's background before getting into specific details. Keep in mind that if you are using a translator, the presentation can take up to three times as long as you would expect otherwise.

Following the presentation, don't expect your Chinese colleagues to ask questions or make comments about what you said. And don't expect any immediate decisions. Your Chinese audience has been listening to what was presented; they will then pass that information on to others in the company and your proposal will be discussed. It's always a good idea to distribute notes on the presentation to your audience. This can be done on the following day, if necessary, but it will help facilitate comprehension and discussion within the Chinese company.

If you will be making a public speech, even if it is to employees of your company, you will also need to tread carefully. When the general manager of a Chinese company, or other high official, makes a speech, it is a serious and formal occasion. It is especially inappropriate to begin a formal speech with a joke or humorous anecdote. A public speech is also not the forum for delivering bad news. For example, if you give a state-of-the-company speech to employees, you would not begin by admitting the company's mistakes or mentioning the unfortunate need for layoffs. If your speech or presentation includes audience members outside of the company, it is best to concentrate on the positive or at the very least, innocuous.

It is always advisable to ask a Chinese colleague to review your presentation or speech beforehand, especially those for more formal occasions. Note, however, that you may have to take care to get a real opinion from your colleague, since he or she may be unwilling to criticize you. It will help if you can ask specific questions rather than requesting a general opinion.

BUSINESS ENTERTAINING

Entertaining is an integral part of Chinese business. It is used as an opportunity to both build and nurture relationships. And since, as this book has so often stressed, relationships are the linchpin of successful business, knowing when, whom, and how to entertain is a skill you cannot do without.

Business entertainment can be a lunch or dinner. And in some southern cities, such as Guangzhou, business breakfasts are gaining popularity. It is highly unusual for business entertaining to take place in a private home. Instead there are a variety of entertainment centers, clubs, hotels, and restaurant facilities that can be used to entertain your Chinese colleagues. Musical shows or karaoke are available in most of the places and many have brochures detailing their services.

While the majority of business entertaining takes the form of a dinner and evening of entertainment, such as karaoke or bowling, don't make the mistake of trying to talk business during this time. Use the time instead to get to know your business partners and establish a friendship.

There are a few notable exceptions to the above guidelines. For example, if you are attending a business lunch with a few people, it may be acceptable to bring up a point of business. However, you should still expect that the lunch will largely be social.

Be sure you take part in the events of an evening of business entertainment as well. Enjoy the meal, make your share of toasts, and don't turn down an invitation to take your shot at the karaoke microphone. The latter activity—getting up and singing in front of people—may either make you break out in hives of embarrassment or seem to you to be too silly for words, but you are being a poor sport if you decline. After all, karaoke has nothing to do with being able to carry a tune or knowing the words to a song. It's all about having fun and joining in the revelry. Nobody likes a wet blanket, least of all the Chinese.

Other possible activities, especially appropriate for higher-ranking individuals, are a weekend game of tennis or golf, if you know someone likes to play. And keep in mind that, with the exception of a celebration banquet, most business entertaining tends to be relatively informal. Spouses are generally not invited.

Who will host—and therefore pay for—the business entertainment is usually clearly expressed. If you issue an invitation, you will pay. It is important to reciprocate hosting duties, even if you are visiting the country. It's a good idea to plan on hosting a dinner just prior to your departure.

If you are hosting a business dinner or lunch, engage in a little bargaining with the restaurant or club beforehand. If you call ahead, you can often arrange a very attractive price for a large party.

Banquet Etiquette

Chinese business banquets require serious attention to detail and a large helping of proper protocol. Most Chinese do not entertain at home, especially for business purposes. Therefore, most entertaining is done in restaurants. If you are invited to a Chinese home, treat it as the great honor it is, but do not feel slighted if it does not happen.

Banquets are a major part of building and maintaining relationships in China. You will almost certainly be invited to one. If you are in China for any length of time, you will also have the occasion to host one.

Guests arrive on time for banquets, not early or late. If you are hosting, be sure to arrive fifteen to thirty minutes early. If your team or group has been invited to a banquet, it is better all around if you arrive as a group. This allows your Chinese hosts to greet everyone properly as protocol demands—according to rank. Latecomers generally throw a monkey wrench into the intricate workings of the protocol of the occasion.

Seating at a banquet is very exact. Where one sits is based on title and seniority. For more formal occasions, name cards delineate the seating arrangements; in less formal circumstances, you will be directed to your seat by your host. Therefore, when you are invited to attend a banquet, wait to be shown to your seat. If you are the host, be sure to get advice from a Chinese colleague to ensure proper seating arrangements and be sure to fulfill your role in seating your guests.

If there is a guest of honor, he or she should be seated opposite the door. If you are the host, the highest-ranking person should be at your right; the second highest-ranking person on your left.

Your place setting will include chopsticks and a porcelain spoon. If you are not familiar with chopsticks, try to learn; it will be greatly appreciated. In larger restaurants you may be able to request a fork; however, Western silverware is often not available outside of large cities and in small restaurants. Use the spoon only for soup. When you aren't using your chopsticks, place them on the chopstick rest, if one is available, or on the table. NEVER stick them upright in the your rice bowl, which is reminiscent of a funeral ritual, or balance them on your rice bowl, considered bad luck.

Refusing food is rude. If you are offered something you don't want, try to take a few bites anyway. In addition, leaving an empty plate may offend your host as it can be taken as a sign that there was not enough to eat. On the other hand, leaving your bowl untouched is also rude. So you should leave some food on your plate, but be sure you've taken a few bites of everything.

If there are bones or seeds, place them on a separate plate, if one is provided, or on the table, not in your rice bowl. Use the sauces for dipping; do not pour them into your rice bowl. Don't drum or tap your chopsticks on the table. You wouldn't use your silverware as drumsticks, would you? In order to use your chopsticks more effectively, lift your rice bowl close to your mouth.

Dinner at a restaurant with more than four people almost always involves several dishes that are placed on a lazy susan in the center of the table for everyone to share. Turn the food clockwise. Wait for the host to serve himself or herself first. Thereafter you can feel free to help yourself. Wait for the host to begin eating before you begin.

Hot tea is served with the meal. If you do not wish to have any more poured for you, simply leave some in your cup. Both non-alcoholic (Coke, juice, soda) and alcoholic beverages (wine, whiskey) will probably be available. You can ask for a non-alcoholic drink if you don't see any on the table. You can ask for bottled water, for which you will be charged. Drinks, such as soda, do not come with ice. If you request ice, the restaurant may or may not have it. In some restaurants the ice may be made from tap water, which has wreaked havoc on many a traveler's stomach. You can generally expect the ice in nicer restaurants to be okay. Beer is not generally served at a formal dinner. However, you can ask for one at an informal dinner.

Chinese have a saying: "Drink more, deeper friendship." Toasting and drinking are a big part of Chinese meals, especially formal ones. Chinese, however, typically drink more than is customary for the average American. You can participate in the toasting with wine or a soft drink instead of whiskey, and without draining your glass each time (See page 193 for this distinction). If you do not drink alcohol, you can plead a medical condition or "doctor's orders."

Toasts are given throughout the meal. They can be in honor of the group or an individual. When you are the toaster, you can safely toast to things like friendship between your respective companies or countries, successful business partnerships, or building a lasting relationship.

Be careful about offering toasts, especially at a business function. The traditional toast of *gānbēi* means "bottoms up" and comes with the expectation that you drain your glass. As an alternative, consider *suí-yì*, which is more along the lines of "Please feel free" and allows you to sip your drink instead.

Fruit is served at the end of the meal. The host will usually signal the end of the banquet by rising to leave. If you need to leave but the host hasn't risen, it is acceptable to leave about ten minutes after the hot towels have been handed around.

MANAGING

American managers typically find that their Chinese subordinates require—and expect—more hands-on attention. The hierarchical structure inherent to the Chinese business environment means that lower level employees are not accustomed to making decisions. Chinese workers typically receive explicit instructions from their supervisor, which they do not question. Even if an employee disagrees with your decision, it is unlikely that he or she will not come out and tell you this.

Language and cultural differences can be difficult hurdles for managers new to China. It is important to establish a mutual trust with your Chinese subordinates and colleagues. This is not accomplished quickly, and it is an on-going process. However, a positive work environment will encourage your Chinese subordinates to help you understand their culture and ways of working.

Try to open the channels of communication as soon as you arrive. Take time to get to know each of the people on your team. You might want to invite them each to lunch in turn to set a foundation for your relationship. Just take care not to appear to exclude anyone; this can easily be construed as implicit criticism.

Face is very important to Chinese. Unfortunately, the Western style of communication and management does not mesh well with the indirect approach required to maintain face. It takes a considerable amount of concentration to ensure that harmony is maintained. The desire to maintain face will impact you in many ways. Here are a few observations and tips on face:

- Never criticize a subordinate in public, as it would cause him or her to lose face.
- Never show your anger or lose your temper; this reflects poorly on you and causes loss of face.
- Don't put people on the spot. They will lose face if they do not know the answer to your question.
- Chinese employees are usually not comfortable asking questions or responding to your comments in front of others. Questioning a supervisor or offering a different opinion would cause loss of face for the superior, and is to be avoided.
- Offer praise to the group as a team and to individuals privately. Singling out an individual in public can have repercussions. The individual may be embarrassed and others may feel that they are being indirectly reprimanded.

It is often preferable to closely supervise your subordinates and continually confirm understanding until you are comfortable working together. Help your subordinates prioritize their tasks. It is often helpful to explain why something is important and needs to take precedence over other tasks they might have. If you have not made it clear that a task should be done immediately, you may not get it when you want it.

Traditionally, diligence and obedience were the most important qualities in a subordinate. This is changing, however, and initiative and creativity are qualities sought by many employers, especially in the private sector, in light of increased competition.

Foreign managers in China now find themselves in a position of bridging the old ways and the new. Most Chinese are open to new ways of working, as long as they can see the benefit and the right approach is used. While change does not come over night, it is possible, with patience and perseverance, to blend the best qualities of the Chinese and Western management styles to mold a team that takes advantage of both ways of doing business. An effective manager could be defined as someone who

- issues clear instruction.
- offers moderate supervision.
- encourages communication and cooperation.
- recognizes the accomplishments of subordinates.
- rewards performance (preferably financially).

LEAVING A LEGACY

Many Americans find it difficult to understand just how important it is to establish positive relationships with a Chinese company. It may help to remember that you are creating a legacy that will benefit—or haunt—your company for many years to come. Visitors to China have found, to their bewilderment, that they were not well received. Meetings could not be scheduled, people could not be reached, and a trip was wasted because the previous visit by the company had damaged relations between the two companies. Americans have a hard time accepting that the actions of someone else can have such a dramatic impact on them, even if that other person or the previous business was unrelated to the business currently at hand.

The reverse is true as well, of course. If other representatives from your company have made a favorable impression on the Chinese, you will find yourself the recipient of special attention and doors that might otherwise remain shut are likely to open. What it boils down to is that you are not just a representative of your company; you are in essence your company and the way that you comport yourself and the relationships you cultivate will affect your company's reputation and reception on a long-term scale.

Tears in the fabric of the business relationship caused by one person can be very difficult to mend.

A NOTE ON USING INTERPRETERS

Although English is now being widely taught in school, it is unrealistic to expect that your Chinese hosts will speak English. Younger Chinese who do speak English are not generally in positions of authority; older people in positions of authority usually do not speak English. Even if they do, they may not be comfortable relying on their English skills to conduct important business.

An interpreter can be one of your best resources while in China. An interpreter who is either bi-cultural or is knowledgeable about the cultural differences between China and the United States can provide you not only with linguistic services but also with invaluable information about protocol, the nuances of Chinese culture, and the interpretation not only of words but also of nonverbal cues and hidden meanings.

While it may seem easier to let your Chinese hosts provide an interpreter—after all, it will be one less thing on a very long list to worry about—you should carefully consider the possible impact of that option. Absolutely objective interpreters are hard to come by; the interpreter's loyalty is most likely going to be toward his or her employer. Selecting your own interpreter ensures that your interests will be looked after. Even if your hosts are providing interpretive services, bringing your own interpreter will help verify the content of the exchange.

It is possible to locate an interpreter once you have arrived in China, but it is sometimes desirable to include your interpreter in the team coming from the United States. Interpreters trained in China may or may not have had any experience in the United States and would therefore be of limited cultural assistance.

Whenever possible, use an interpreter who is familiar with your industry and even with your company. If your company does not have access to a suitable individual and must hire someone unfamiliar to you or your company, arrange to meet with the interpreter before the meetings in order to brief him on your company, your goals, and your expectations. Provide the interpreter with as much documentation as possible to allow him to prepare for the meeting.

If you happen to have a Chinese-speaking team member and are relying on that person to interpret for the team, don't also expect him or her to enter into the negotiations. It not only becomes confusing, it is virtually impossible, because interpreting requires a great deal of focus and concentration. So if any key member or members of your team speaks Chinese, it is still wise to have an official interpreter who is not part of the actual negotiation.

If you are new to using interpreters, here are some guidelines.

- If each team has an interpreter present, each will translate the comments of his or her respective team. If only one is present, he will obviously be responsible for all translation.
- Always address the person to whom the comment or question is directed, not the interpreter. This takes practice, as most people tend to automatically turn to face the interpreter.
- Don't overwhelm the interpreter with words. You should pause for interpretation after every two or three sentences.
- Try to keep your sentences as uncomplicated as possible. A long, rambling sentence is very difficult to translate.
- Keep your vocabulary as simple as the situation will allow. Hopefully you will have taken the time to ensure that the interpreter has a vocabulary compatible with your needs, and will have gone over any technical details with him or her.
- Avoid slang and colloquialisms. They may not be understood or, potentially even more disastrous, misunderstood if they are interpreted literally.
- The interpreter is not a machine. Interpreting takes an enormous amount of mental energy and is very draining. Allow at least a brief rest period after every hour or so. This is another argument in favor of having separate interpreters.
- If you are having trouble making yourself understood—and this goes for direct communication as well as interpreter-assisted communication—do not under any circumstance repeat your question or comment in ever-increasing volume. The problem is comprehension, not hearing. Rephrase the statement until you reach understanding.

EIGHT

LAST NOTES

We hope that this book has given you some insight into China and has suggested some ways to prepare yourself for a successful, rewarding experience. The practical tips contained in this book should help you feel more comfortable as your journey begins, and the information on the Chinese culture will help you navigate as your journey continues. Finally, you'll find a language section that contains the most essential words and phrases; remember that even a little bit of Chinese will make a world of difference.

In addition to the specific information covered in these seven chapters, don't forget these important guidelines for cross-cultural interaction anywhere around the globe:

- Learn about the culture you are visiting. The better you understand their culture, the more prepared you will be to tune your skills to their frequency.
- Keep your sense of humor. Things are guaranteed to go wrong now and again, and you will make mistakes. Your best defense is your ability to find humor in the situation.
- And finally, respect other cultures. Just because it's not the way you do things doesn't mean it's wrong.

Good luck in the exciting new environment that awaits you in China.

NINE

LANGUAGE NOTES

CHINESE PRONUNCIATION

CONSONANTS

Chinese	English Equivalent	Chinese	English Equivalent
b	boat	p	pass
m	mouse	f	flag
d	dock	t	tongue
n	nest	l	life
g	goat	k	keep
h	house	j	and yet
q	chicken	x	short
zh	judge	ch	church
sh	sheep	r*	read
z	seeds	c	dots
s	seed		

VOWELS

Chinese	English Equivalent	Chinese	English Equivalent
ü	you	ia	yard
üe	you + e	ian	yen
a	father	iang	young
ai	kite	ie	yet
ao	now	o	all
e	earn	ou	go
ei	day	u	wood
er	curve	ua	waft
i	yield	uo	wall
i (after z, c, s, zh, ch, sh)	thunder		

THE CHINESE LANGUAGE

WORD ORDER

The basic Chinese sentence structure is the same as in English, following the pattern of subject-verb-object:

He took my pen.   Tā ná le wǒ de bǐ.
 s   v   o   s   v   o

NOUNS

There are no articles in Chinese, although there are many "counters," which are used when a certain number of a given noun is specified. Various attributes of a noun—such as size, shape, or use—determine which counter is used with that noun. Chinese does not distinguish between singular and plural.

a pen   yìzhī bǐ
a book   yìběn shū

VERBS

Chinese verbs are not conjugated, and they do not have tenses. Instead, a system of word order, word repetition, and the addition of a number of adverbs serves to indicate the tense of a verb, whether the verb is a suggestion or an order, or even whether the verb is part of a question. *Tā zài ná wǒ de bǐ.* (He is taking my pen.) *Tā ná le wǒ de bǐ.* (He took my pen.) *Tā yǒu méi yǒu ná wǒ de bǐ?* (Did he take my pen?) *Tā yào ná wǒ de bǐ.* (He will take my pen.)

TONES

In English, intonation patterns can indicate whether a sentence is a statement (He's hungry.), a question (He's hungry?), or an exclamation (He's hungry!). Entire sentences carry particular "tones," but individual words do not. In Chinese, words have a particular tone value, and these tones are important in determining the meaning of a word. Observe the meanings of the following examples, each said with one of the four tones found in standard Chinese: *mā* (high, steady tone): mother, *má* (rising tone, like a question): fiber, *mǎ* (dipping tone): horse, and *mà* (dropping tone): swear.

PHRASES

You don't need to master the entire Chinese language to spend a week in China, but taking charge of a few key phrases in the language can aid you in just getting by. The following supplement will allow you to get a hotel room, get around town, order a drink at the end of the day, and get help in case of an emergency.

Listen to the phrase and repeat what you hear in the space provided.

COMMON GREETINGS

Hello/Good morning.	Nǐ hǎo/Zǎoshàng hǎo.
Good evening.	Wǎnshàng hǎo.
Good-bye.	Zàijiàn.

Title for a married woman or an older unmarried woman	Tàitai/Fūrén
Title for a young and unmarried woman	Xiǎojiě
Title for a man	Xiānshēng
How are you?	Nǐ hǎo ma?
Fine, thanks. And you?	Hěn hǎo. Xièxie. Nǐ ne?
What is your name?	Nǐ jiào shénme míngzi?
My name is . . .	Wǒ jiào . . .
Nice to meet you.	Hěn gāoxìng rènshì nǐ.
I'll see you later.	Huítóu jiàn.

POLITE EXPRESSIONS

Please.	Qǐng.
Thank you.	Xièxiè.
Thank you very much.	Fēicháng gǎnxiè.
You're welcome.	Bú yòng xiè.
Yes, thank you.	Shì de, Xièxiè.
No, thank you.	Bù, xièxiè.
I beg your pardon.	Qǐng yuánliàng.
I'm sorry.	Hěn baòqiàn.

Pardon me.	Dùibùqǐ.
That's okay.	Méi shénme.
It doesn't matter.	Méi guānxi.
Do you speak English?	Nǐ shūo Yīngyǔ ma?
Yes.	Shì de.
No.	Bù.
Maybe.	Huòxǔ.

I can speak a little.	Wǒ néng shūo yī diǎnr.
I understand a little.	Wǒ dǒng yì diǎnr.
I don't understand.	Wǒ bù dǒng.
I don't speak Chinese very well.	Wǒ Zhōngwén shūo de bù hǎo.
Would you repeat that, please?	Qǐng zài shūo yíbiàn?
I don't know.	Wǒ bù zhīdaò.

No problem.	Méi wèntí.
It's my pleasure.	Lèyì er wéi.

NEEDS AND QUESTION WORDS

I'd like . . .	Wǒ xiǎng . . .
I need . . .	Wǒ xūyào . . .
What would you like?	Nǐ yaò shénme?
Please bring me . . .	Qǐng gěi wǒ . . .
I'm looking for . . .	Wǒ zài zhǎo . . .
I'm hungry.	Wǒ è le.
I'm thirsty	Wǒ kǒukě
It's important.	Hěn zhòngyào.
It's urgent.	Hěn jǐnjí.
How?	Zěnmeyàng?
How much?	Duōshǎo?
How many?	Duōshǎo gè?
Which?	Nǎ yí gè?
What?	Shénme?
What kind of?	Shénme yàng de?
Who?	Shuí?
Where?	Nǎli?
When?	Shénme shíhòu?
What does this mean?	Zhè shì shénme yìsi?
What does that mean?	Nà shì shénme yìsi?
How do you say . . . in Chinese?	. . . yòng Zhōngwén zěnme shūo?

AT THE AIRPORT

Where is . . .	. . . zài nǎr?
customs?	Hǎigūan
passport control?	Hùzhào jiǎnyàn
the information booth?	Wènxùntái
the ticketing counter?	Shòupiàochù
the baggage claim?	Xínglǐchù
the ground transportation?	Dìmìan jiāotōng

LANGUAGE NOTES

Is there a bus service to the city?	Yǒu qù chéng lǐ de gōnggòng qìchē ma?

Where are . . .	. . . zài nǎr?
the international departures?	Guójì hángbān chūfā diǎn
the international arrivals?	Guójì hángbān dàodá diǎn

What is your nationality?	Nǐ shì něi guó rén?
I am an American.	Wǒ shì Měiguó rén.
I am Canadian.	Wǒ shì Jiānádà rén.

AT THE HOTEL, RESERVING A ROOM

I would like a room.	Wǒ yào yí ge fángjiān.
for one person	dānrén fáng
for two people	shuāngrén fáng
for tonight	jīntīan wǎnshàng
for two nights	liǎng gè wǎnshàng
for a week	yí ge xīngqī

Do you have a different room?	Nǐ hái yǒu bié de fángjiān ma?
with a bath	dài yùshì de fángjiān
with a shower	dài línyù de fángjiān
with a toilet	dài cèsuǒ de fángjiān
with air-conditioning	yǒu kōngtiáo de fángjiān
How much is it?	Duōshǎo qián?
My bill, please.	Qǐng jiézhàng.

AT THE RESTAURANT

Where can we find a good restaurant?	Zài nǎr kěyǐ zhǎodào yìjiā hǎo cānguǎn?
We'd like a(n) . . . restaurant.	Wǒmen xiǎng qù yì gè . . . cānguǎn.

elegant	gāo jí
fast-food	kuàicān
inexpensive	piányì de
seafood	hǎixiān
vegetarian	sùshí

Café	Kāfeī diàn
A table for two	Liǎng wèi
Waiter, a menu please.	Fúwùyuán, qǐng gěi wǒmen càidān.
The wine list, please.	Qǐng gěi wǒmen jiǔdān.
Appetizers	Kāiwèi shíwù
Main course	Zhǔ cài
Dessert	Tiándiǎn
What would you like?	Nǐ yào shénme cài?
What would you like to drink?	Nǐ yào hē shénme yǐnliào?
Can you recommend a good wine?	Nǐ néng tūijiàn yí ge hǎo jiǔ ma?
Wine, please.	Qǐng lǎi diǎn jiǔ.
Beer, please.	Qǐng lǎi diǎn píjiǔ.
I didn't order this.	Wǒ méiyǒu diǎn zhè gè.
That's all, thanks.	Jiù zhèxie, xièxiè.
The check, please.	Qǐng jiézhàng.
Cheers!/Bottoms Up! To your health!	Gānbēi! Zhù nǐ shēntì jiànkāng.

OUT ON THE TOWN

Where can I find . . .	Nǎr yǒu ...
an art museum?	yìshù bówùguǎn?
a museum of natural history?	zìrán lìshī bówùguǎn?
a history museum?	lìshī bówuguǎn?
a gallery?	huàláng?
interesting architecture?	yǒuqù de jiànzhùwù?
a church?	jiàotáng?
the zoo?	dòngwùyuán?
I'd like . . .	Wǒ xiǎng

to see a play.	kàn xì.
to see a movie.	kàn diànyǐng.
to see a concert.	qù yīnyuèhuì.
to see the opera.	kàn gējù.
to go sightseeing.	qù guānguāng.
to go on a bike ride.	qí dānchē.

SHOPPING

Where is the best place to go shopping for . . .	Mǎi...zuì hǎo qù nǎr?
clothes?	yīfu
food?	shíwù
souvenirs?	jìniànpǐn
furniture?	jīajù
fabric?	bùliào
antiques?	gǔdǒng
books?	shūjí
sporting goods?	yùndòng wùpǐn
electronics?	diànqì
computers?	diànnǎo

DIRECTIONS

Excuse me. Where is . . .	Duìbùqǐ...zài nǎr?
the bus stop?	Qìchēzhàn
the subway station?	Dìtiězhàn
the rest room?	Xǐ shǒujiān
the taxi stand?	Chūzū chēzhàn
the nearest bank?	Zùijìn de yínháng
the hotel?	Lǚguǎn
To the right	Zài yòubiān.

To the left.	Zài zuǒbiān.
Straight ahead.	Wǎng qián zhízǒu.
It's near here.	Jiùzài zhè fùjìn.
Go back.	Wǎng húi zǒu.
Next to ...	Jìnkào ...

NUMBERS

Cardinal

0	Líng	19	Shíjǐu
1	Yī	20	Ershí
2	Er	21	Ershíyī
3	Sān	22	Ershí'èr
4	Sì	23	Eshísān
5	Wǔ	30	Sānshí
6	Lìu	40	Sìshí
7	Qī	50	Wǔshí
8	Bā	60	Lìushí
9	Jǐu	70	Qīshí
10	Shí	80	Bāshí
11	Shíyī	90	Jǐushí
12	Shí'èr	100	Yìbǎi
13	Shísān	1,000	Yìqiān
14	Shísì	1,100	Yìqiān yìbǎi
15	Shíwǔ	2,000	Liǎngqiān
16	Shílìu	10,000	Yíwàn
17	Shíqī	100,000	Shíwàn
18	Shíbā	1,000,000	Bǎiwàn

Ordinal

first	Dì yī	seventeenth	Dì shíqī
second	Dì èr	eighteenth	Dì shíbā
third	Dì sān	nineteenth	Dì shíjǐu
fourth	Dì sì	twentieth	Dì èrshí
fifth	Dì wǔ	twenty-first	Dì èrshíyī
sixth	Dì lìu	twenty-second	Dì èrshí'èr
seventh	Dì qi	thirtieth	Dì sānshí
eighth	Dì bā	fortieth	Dì sìshí
ninth	Dì jǐu	fiftieth	Dì wǔshí
tenth	Dì shí	sixtieth	Dì lìushí
eleventh	Dì shíyī	seventieth	Dì qīshí
twelfth	Dì shí'èr	eightieth	Dì bāshí
thirteenth	Dì shísān	ninetieth	Dì jǐushí
fourteenth	Dì shísì	hundredth	Dì yìbǎi
fifteenth	Dì shíwǔ	thousandth	Dì yìqiān
sixteenth	Dì shílìu		

TIME

What time is it?	Xiànzài shénme shíjiān?
It is noon.	Zhōngwǔ.
It is midnight.	Bànyè.
It is 9:00 A.M.	Shàngwǔ jǐu diǎn.
It is 1:00 P.M.	Xiàwǔ yì diǎn.
It is 3 o'clock.	Sān diǎn (zhōng).
5:15	Wǔ diǎn shíwǔ fēn.
7:30	Qī diǎn sānshí (bàn).
9:45	Jǐu diǎn sìshíwǔ.

Now	Xiànzài
Later	Wǎn yì diǎnr
Immediately	Mǎshàng
Soon	Hěn kuài

Monday	Xīngqī yī
Tuesday	Xīngqī èr
Wednesday	Xīngqī sān
Thursday	Xīngqī sì
Friday	Xīngqī wǔ
Saturday	Xīngqī liù
Sunday	Xīngqī rì (tiān)

| **What day is today?** | Jīntiān shì xīngqī jǐ? |

January	Yí yuè
February	Èr yuè
March	Sān yuè
April	Sì yuè
May	Wǔ yuè
June	Liù yuè
July	Qī yuè
August	Bā yuè
September	Jiǔ yuè
October	Shí yuè
November	Shíyī yuè
December	Shí'èr yùe

| **What is the date today?** | Jīntiān shì shénme rìzi? |

| **Today is Thursday, September 22.** | Jīntiān shì jiǔ yuè èrshí'èr hào, xīngqī sì. |

| **Yesterday was Wednesday, September 21.** | Zuǒtiān shì jiǔ yùe èrshíyī hào, xīngqī sān. |

| **Tomorrow is Friday, September 23.** | Míngtiān shì jiǔ yuè èrshísān hào, xīngqī wǔ. |

MODERN CONNECTIONS

Where can I find . . .	Zài nǎr kěyǐ shǐ yòng . . .
a telephone?	diànhuà?
a fax machine?	chuánzhēnjī?
an Internet connection?	guójì wǎnglù?
How do I call the United States?	Gěi Měiguó dǎ diànhuà zěnme dǎ?
I need . . .	Wǒ xūyào . . .
a fax sent.	fā chuánzhēn.
a hookup to the Internet.	yǔ guójì wǎnglù liánjiē.
a computer.	diànnǎo.
a package sent overnight.	liányè bǎ bāoguǒ jìchū.
some copies made.	fùyìn yìxiē wénjiàn.
a VCR and monitor.	lùyǐngjī he xiǎnshiqì.
an overhead projector and markers.	huàndēngjī he biāoshìqì.

EMERGENCIES AND SAFETY

Help!	Jiùmìng a!
Fire!	Jiùhuǒ a!
I need a doctor.	Wǒ yào kàn yīshēng.
Call an ambulance!	Mǎshàng jiào jiùhùchē!
What happened?	Fāshēng le shénme shì?
I am/My wife is/My husband is/ My friend is/Someone is . . .	Wǒ/Wǒ qīzi/Wǒ Zhàngfu/ Wǒ péngyǒu/Yǒu rén . . .
very sick.	bìng de hěn lìhài.
having a heart attack.	xīnzàngbìng fāzuò le.
choking.	yēzhù le.
losing consciousness.	yūndǎo le.
about to vomit.	yào ǒutù le.
having a seizure.	yòu fābìng le.
stuck.	bèi kǎ zhù le.

I can't breathe.	Wǒ bù néng hūxī.
I tripped and fell.	Wǒ bàn dǎo le.
I cut myself.	Wǒ gē shāng le.
I drank too much.	Wǒ jǐu hē de tài duō le.
I don't know.	Wǒ bù zhīdào.
I've injured my...	Wǒ de . . . shòushāng le.
head	tóu
neck	bózi
back	bèi
arm	shǒubèi
leg	tuǐ
foot	jiǎo
eye(s)	yǎnjīng
I've been robbed.	Wǒ bèi qiǎng le.

BEFORE YOU GO

Passports. Be sure that each member of your family has one, and that each is valid for the length of your assignment. Children should have separate passports; otherwise they will not be allowed to travel alone or with an adult other than their parents, even in an emergency.

Visas. Check with the embassy of any countries you will be in for necessary visas. Requirements vary by country, especially for international relocation. As you travel, don't overlook the fact that some countries require a transit visa for people passing through the country, even if you don't get off your plane or train.

Vaccinations/inoculations. Check for recommended vaccinations or inoculations for the country you will be living in, as well as any countries you intend to visit. (This is listed on the U.S. Department of State Consular Information Sheet; see Travel advisories on page 217.) The Department of Health and Human Services' Office of Public Health Services is able to issue an International Certificate of Vaccination containing your personal history of vaccinations. The ICV is approved by the World Health Organization.

Insurance. Make sure that your insurance will cover you while you are abroad. Check now, before you need it. If it won't, do some research to find out how to supplement or change your insurance so that you are adequately covered.

International driver's permits. Although you can use your U.S. or Canadian driver's license in some countries, it is generally advisable to obtain an international driver's permit. This is available from AAA for a small fee and does not require taking a test. International driver's permits are valid for one year; after that time, you may have to get a local driver's license. Be sure that you get a permit that is valid for the country(ies) that you will be driving in.

Pets. Check with the consulate of your host country to find out about restrictions and requirements for bringing pets into the country. Most countries require a health and immunization certificate from a veterinarian; some have quarantine periods upon arrival.

Medical records. Obtain complete medical records for each member of your family. Have one copy on hand for the trip in case of an emergency.

Prescriptions and medication. If you or anyone in your family takes prescription medication, especially those containing narcotics, have your doctor give you a letter stating what the drug is and why it is necessary. Be sure you get a list of the Latin name of all prescription drugs from your doctor, since brand names vary from country to country. Take a six-month supply of any prescription medication, if possible. All medication, prescription or over-the-counter, should be in its original bottle and clearly labeled. Drug and narcotics laws are very strict in many countries, and you do not want to run afoul of them. Ask your dentist if it is advisable to have fluoride treatments, especially for children; most countries do not add fluoride to the water.

School records. If you have chosen a school for your child, you will probably have already made arrangements to forward your child's records. If not, be sure to request a complete set of records to take with you for each child. Don't forget school records, including diplomas and certificates, for yourself or your partner if either one of you might take continuing education classes while you're abroad!

Wills and guardianships. Your personal affairs should be in order before you leave. Your lawyer or a family member should have access to these documents in the case of an emergency.

Power of attorney. Assign power of attorney to act in your interest at home, if necessary. (A power of attorney does not have to be permanent and can be nullified when you return, if desired.)

Paying bills. If you've got a mortgage or other payments that must be paid while you're abroad, decide how to handle them before you go. There are several options, including maintaining a checking account at home and paying bills yourself, arranging for your bank to pay them (not all banks offer this service), or having your lawyer, accountant or a family member pay them.

Travel advisories. The U.S. Department of State publishes a one to two page consular information sheet on each country that covers basic topics such as medical and safety information, as well as addresses and phone numbers of U.S. consulates in the country. When necessary, travel advisories are released regarding areas of political instability, terrorist activity, etc. Check before you travel. (Consular information sheets and travel advisories are also available on many on-line services, such as CompuServe, and at the State Department Web site at http://www.state.gov.)

Copy of important documents. Make two copies of important documents; take one with you and leave one with your lawyer or a family member. Important documents include:

- Passport (the inside front cover, which contains your passport number and other information)
- Visas, transit visas, and tourist cards
- Driver's license, international driving permit
- Insurance card and other information
- International Certificate of Vaccination, medical records

Special needs. If you or anyone in your family has any special needs, check that appropriate facilities and services are available from hotels and airlines. Not all are equipped to deal with infants, persons with physical disabilities, and other concerns such as medication that requires special handling or refrigeration.

Change of address. Be sure to inform all of the necessary people and companies of your change of address. Some companies will assess a service fee for mailing bills and statements internationally. Write to each company, and keep a copy of the notice in case a problem develops and to remind you what bills and statements you should be receiving. Don't forget the following:

- Banks where you are keeping local accounts or have loans
- Credit cards, including department store and gasoline cards
- Stockbroker or stock transfer agent, retirement account agents
- Lawyer
- Accountant
- Insurance company, including homeowners, personal, medical and life
- Tax offices in any city or state where you have property tax liabilities
- Voter registration office
- Magazines and periodicals
- Alumni association and professional memberships

Bank letter of reference. It is often difficult to establish banking services in a country where you have no credit history. It will help to have your bank or credit card write you a letter of good credit. Also helpful is a letter from your local office in your new country that states your salary. Some banks now have branches in many countries; you may be able to open an expatriate account at home before you go that will allow you access to bank services worldwide.

Close unnecessary accounts. However, you should leave open one or two key accounts that will provide you with a credit history when you return. Also make arrangements to terminate telephone, utility, garbage collection, newspaper delivery, and other services as necessary.

Inventory. An inventory of all of your belongings is helpful for shipping and insurance purposes. Enlist the help of an appraiser as necessary for items of value.

Packing. Put a card with your name and address inside each piece of luggage and each box being shipped. Don't put your passport in the boxes to be shipped!!

CONTACTS &
RESOURCES

BUSINESS AND INFORMATION RESOUCES

Embassy of the People's Republic of China

2300 Connecticut Avenue NW
Washington, DC 20008
Tel: (202) 328–2500

*Consulate General of the
People's Republic of China*

520 12th Avenue
New York, NY 10036
Tel: (212) 868–7752

1450 Laguna Street
San Francisco, CA 94115
Tel: (415) 563–4885

3417 Montrose Blvd.
Houston, TX 77006
Tel: (713) 524–4311

100 West Erie St.
Chicago, IL 60610
Tel: (312) 803–0098

502 Shatto Place, Suite 300
Los Angeles, CA 90020
Tel: (213) 807–8088

American Embassy Beijing

Xiu Shui Bei Jie 3
Beijing 100600
People's Republic of China
Tel: (86) (1) 6532–3831
Fax: (86) (1) 6532–3178
*In addition to the U.S. embassy in Beijing, there are
U.S. Consulates General in Chengdu, Guangzhou,
Shanghai, and Shenyang.*

SOCIAL AND EXPATRIATE RESOURCES

Beijing

The American Club of Beijing

Lido Club, Holiday Inn Lido
Tel: 6437–6743

Beijing International Club

Tel: 6532–5849

Hash House Harriers

Tel: 6532–1961
International Club
Chang An Avenue

International Newcomers Network

Capital Mansions
6 Xin Yuan Nan Road
Tel: 6467–2225

Professional Women's Network

c/o Community Liaison Office
U.S. and Canadian Embassies

Shanghai

Australian Business Club

Australian Consulate
17 Fuxing Xi Rd.

Shanghai Expatriate Society

Tel: 6268–9023 or 6219–8267

RESOURCES FOR MOVING ABROAD

Video Overseas, Inc.

246 8th Avenue
2nd Floor
New York, NY 10011
Tel: (212) 645–0797 or (800) 317–6945
Fax: (212) 242–8144
Web site: www.videooverseas.com
*Household appliances and electronics that are adapted
or manufactured for international use.*

Air Animal, Inc.
(U.S. and Canada)

Tel: (800) 635–3448
*Information and assistance on moving
your pet abroad.*

HELPFUL WEB SITES

Escape Artist

Web site: www.escapeartist.com

Expat Exchange

Web site: www.expatexchange.com

Utopia

Web site: www.utopia-asia.com
Resources and information for gays

TRAVEL IN CHINA

China International Travel Service
U.S. Centers for Disease Control
and Prevention

Atlanta, GA
Tel: 877–FYI–TRIP (877–394–8747)
Web site: www.cdc.gov/travel/index.htm
Health advisories, immunization recommendations or
requirements, and advice on food and drinking water
safety for regions and countries.

CROSS-CULTURAL RESOURCES

Terra Cognita

Web site: www.terracognita.com
Videos, books, audio, and Internet training and resources
for living and working in China and around the world.

METRIC CONVERSIONS

Although a sizing conversion chart can be a step in the right direction, an accurate fit is found only by trying the item on, just as you would at home. Most Westerners despair of not being able to buy clothes off the rack in China, as the Chinese frame is simply smaller than a Western one. Some clothing has metric sizing, the conversions for which follow, although they are merely guidelines.

WOMEN'S DRESSES AND SKIRTS

U.S.	3	5	7	9	11	12	13	14	15	16	18
Continental	36	38	38	40	40	42	42	44	44	46	46
British	8	10	11	12	13	14	15	16	17	18	20
Chinese	34	36	38	40	42	44					

WOMEN'S BLOUSES AND SWEATERS

U.S.	4	6	8	10	12	14	16	18	20	22	24
Continental	32	34	36	38	40	42	44	46	48	50	52
British	26	28	30	32	34	36	38	40	42	44	46

WOMEN'S SHOES

U.S.	5	6	7	8	9	10
Continental	36	37	38	39	40	41
British	3½	4½	5½	6½	7½	8½

MEN'S SUITS

U.S.	34	36	38	40	42	44	46	48
Continental	44	46	48	50	52	54	56	58
British	34	36	38	40	42	44	46	48

MEN'S SHIRTS

U.S.	14½	15	15½	16	16½	17	17½	18
Continental	37	38	39	41	42	43	44	45
British	14½	15	15½	16	16½	17	17½	18

MEN'S SHOES

U.S.	7	8	9	10	11	12	13
Continental	39½	41	42	43	44½	46	47
British	6	7	8	9	10	11	12

CHILDREN'S CLOTHING

U.S.	3	4	5	6	6x
Continental	98	104	110	116	122
British	18	20	22	24	26

CHILDREN'S SHOES

U.S.	8	9	10	11	12	13	1	2	3
Continental	24	25	27	28	29	30	32	33	34
British	7	8	9	10	11	12	13	1	2

TRADITIONAL CHINESE MEASUREMENTS

1 jin (catty)	1.102 pounds
1 dan (picul)	0.492 tons
1 mu	0.1647 acres
1 li	0.311 miles

DISTANCE

1 yard	0.914 meters
1 foot	0.305 meters
1 inch	2.54 centimeters
1 mile	1.609 kilometers
1 meter	1.094 yards
1 meter	3.279 feet
1 centimeter	0.394 inches
1 kilometer	0.622 miles

SPEED

1 mph	1.609 kph
30 mph	48 kph
55 mph	88 kph
65 mph	105 kph
80 mph	128 kph
100 mph	160 kph
1 kph	0.622 mph
55 kph	34 mph
65 kph	40 mph
80 kph	50 mph
100 kph	62 mph
150 kph	93 mph

DRY MEASURES

1 pint	.551 liters
1 quart	1.101 liters
1 liter	0.908 dry quarts

LIQUID MEASURES

1 fluid ounce	29.57 milliliters
1 pint	0.47 liters
1 quart	0.946 liters
1 gallon	3.785 liters
1 liter	1.057 liquid quarts

WEIGHT

1 ounce	28.35 grams
1 pound	0.45 kilograms
1 gram	0.035 ounces
1 kilogram	2.20 pounds

TEMPERATURE

To convert Fahrenheit into Celsius, subtract 32, multiply by 5, and divide by 9.

To convert Celsius into Fahrenheit, multiply by 9, divide by 5, and add 32.

FAHRENHEIT → CELSIUS		CELSIUS → FAHRENHEIT	
-20	-28	-50	-58
-15	-26	-45	-49
-10	-23	-40	-40
5	20	-35	-31
0	-17	-30	-22
5	-15	-25	-13
10	-12	-20	-4
15	-9	-15	5
20	-6	-10	14
25	-3	-5	23
30	-1	0	32
35	1	5	41
40	4	10	50
45	7	15	59
50	10	20	6
55	12	25	77
60	15	30	86
65	18	35	95
70	21	40	104
75	23	45	113
80	26	50	122
85	29	55	131
90	32	60	140
95	35	65	149
100	37	70	158

APPENDIX C: METRIC CONVERSIONS

FAHRENHEIT → CELSIUS		CELSIUS → FAHRENHEIT	
105	40	75	167
110	43	80	176
115	46	85	185
120	48	90	194
125	51	95	203
150	65	100	212
175	79	105	221
200	93	110	230
225	107	115	239
250	121	120	248
275	135	125	257
300	148	150	302
325	162	175	347
350	176	200	392
375	190	225	437
400	204	250	482
425	218	275	527
450	232	300	572
475	246	500	932
500	260		

AAA (American Automobile
    Association), 216
Air pollution, 156, 157
    Air travel. See Public transportation
Appliances, 118, 123, 124–126
Artists, 36–37
ATM (Automated Teller Machine), 138

Banking
    ATM (Automated Teller Machine),
        138
    bill payments, 137–138, 217
    checking account, 137
    credit cards, 134, 137, 138
    currency exchange, 137, 138
    debit cards, 134, 137, 138
    direct deposit, 137
    foreign banks, 137–138, 219
    hours, 138
    letter of reference, 218–219
    savings account, 138
    traveler's checks, 137
Banquet, 178, 180–181, 186–187,
    190–193
Bargaining, 134–135
Benefits, employee, 165–166
Bicycle, 117, 131
Bill payments, 137–138, 217
Blood transfusions, 156–157
Bowing. See Etiquette
Bribery, 150
Buddhism, 41, 42–43
Bus. See Public transportation

Business cards, 174
Business hours, 166
Business relationships, 70–74, 164,
    168–169, 177–178, 181, 195
    initial contacts, 113–114, 172–173

Car
    hiring, 115, 116, 131
    importing, 131
    rental, 115
    See also Driving
Cellular phone. See under Telephone
Change of address, 218
Checks. See Banking
Children
    child care, 98
    clothing, 135
    contact with home, 85, 96–97, 108
    cultural adaptation, 95–97
    household chores, 98
    moving abroad, 83–87, 95–97
    repatriation, 106–107
    school, 132–133
Christianity, 41, 42
Climate, 24
Clothing, 135–136
Communication
    business, 167, 175–177
    cultural differences, 58–61, 147–149
Communism, 39
Communist Party, 40, 48, 164
Computers, 107, 126, 129, 167
Confucianism, 37, 41, 42, 53–54,

Confucianism (cont'd)
   64–65, 68–69, 166
Contact with home, 103–104, 106,
   107–108
  children, 85, 96–97, 108
  professional, 105
Contract, 186
Conversation, 147–149
  business, 174–175
Corporate structure, 161–166
  hierarchy, 164–165, 193–194
  types, 161–163
  worker participation, 164–166
Credit cards, 134, 137, 138
Crime. See Safety
Cultural adaptation
  children, 95–97
  coping techniques, 93
  expatriate clubs, 99, 102–103
  family relationships, 93–94
  four stages, 90–92
  nonworking partner, 94–95
  parenting, 97–98
  persons of color, 101–102
  repatriation, 104–107
  sexual orientation, 102
  single persons, 99–100
  women, 100
Cultural differences, 21–22, 51–52, 79
  communication, 58–61, 147–149
  contracts, 186
  decision-making, 65, 193
  friendships, 139–141
  group dynamics, 62–65
  hierarchy, 66–70, 193–194
  interpersonal relationships, 53–54,
    70–74, 139–141, 147–149
  presentations, 187–189
  reasoning style, 74–78
  status, 67, 69–70
  time, 55–57
  tipping, 115, 160
Culture shock. See Cultural adaptation
Currency, 24, 134, 136–138
Currency exchange, 114, 137, 138
Customs, 111–113, 114, 151

Danwei. See Work unit
Dating, 142

Debit cards, 134, 137, 138
Decision-making, 65, 164–165, 177,
   181–182, 184, 193
Doctor. See Health
Domestic employees, 97
Driving
  car rental, 115
  license, 115, 131–132, 216, 218
  See also Car
Dual-career couples
  child care, 98
  moving abroad, 87–89
Economy, 24
Education (Chinese), 48–50
E-mail, 107, 167, 176–177
Emergency. See Safety
Employment, 24, 162–163, 165–166
  benefits, 165–166
Entertainment, 151–153
  business, 189–193
Ethnic groups, 23, 24–25, 42, 48, 154
Etiquette, 146–147
  business, 174–175
  conversation, 147–149
  table manners, 191–193
Expatriate clubs, 99–100, 102–103

"Face," 59–61, 134–135, 149, 193–194
Family
  cultural adaptation, 93–94
  moving abroad, 82–90, 93–98
Feng shui, 77–78, 145, 146
Finance. See Banking
Flowers, 141
Food, 154, 158
  etiquette, 190–193
  restaurants, 154, 160, 189–193
Formality, 70, 147–148, 174
Forms of address, 70, 147–148
Friendships, 99, 139–141

Geography, 23, 24
Gifts
  business, 149–151, 175, 187
  to host, 141
"Global nomads," 96–97
Government, 37–41
  and business, 163–164, 181–182
Group dynamics, 53–54, 61, 62–65

Guanxi, 72–74
Guest
　in private home, 141–142
　in restaurant, 189–193

Health, 111–112, 155–158
　insurance, 156, 216, 218
Hierarchy, 53–54
　corporate, 164–165, 177, 178–179,
　　181–182, 191, 193–194
　cultural differences, 67–70, 193–194
History, 26–34, 54
Holidays, 44–48
Homosexuality. See Sexual orientation
Hotels, 128, 130, 156, 157, 160
Housing
　fees, 122, 123, 124
　finding, 120–122
　furnishings, 120–121, 123
　residence permit, 119–120
　utilities, 123–124, 126
　See also Telephone
Humor, 149, 188, 189

Immunization, 112, 156, 157, 215, 218
Individualism, 63–64, 65
Infants, 85
Inoculation. See Immunization
Insurance, health, 156, 216, 218
Internet. See under Telephone
Interpreter, 181, 188, 196–197
Islam, 41, 42, 43–44

Language, 23, 109
Leisure time, 139–141

Mail. See Post office
Manager, 162, 163, 164–165, 193–195
Marriage. See Weddings
Measures. See Weights and measures
Medical care. See Health
Medical records, 216, 218
Medicine, 113, 156, 216
Meeting people. See Friendships;
　Social relations
Meetings, 178–181
Metric system, 118
Moving abroad
　banking, 137–138, 218–219

change of address, 218
children, 83–87, 96–97
contact with home, 103, 106,
　107–108
cultural adaptation, 89–103
dual-career couples, 87–89
expatriate clubs, 99–100, 102–103
family, 82–89, 93–98
goals, 82
infants and toddlers, 85
inventory of possessions, 219
language, 109
packing, 84, 124–126, 219
persons of color, 101–102
preparation, 81–83, 108–110,
　199–200
preschoolers, 86, 95, 96
preteens, 86, 95–96, 106–107
sexual orientation, 102
single persons, 99–100
spouse or partner, 82, 87–89
teenagers, 86–87, 95–96, 97,
　106–107
women, 100
See also Contact with home;
　Repatriation
Names, 147–148, 174
Negotiation, 65, 181–187, 197
New Year. See Holidays
Nonworking partner
　cultural adaptation, 94–95
　moving abroad, 87–88
　same-sex couples, 102

Office space, 167

Packing, 84, 124–126, 219
Pager, 127–128
Parenting abroad
　child care, 98
　cultural adaptation, 97–98
Partner. See Spouse
Passport, 118, 215, 218
Persons of color, 101–102
Pets, 129–131, 216
Philosophers, 37
Political figures, historical, 34–36
Politics. See Government
Pollution. See Air pollution

Population, 23. *See also* Ethnic groups
Post office, 128, 159–160
Power of attorney, 217
Preschoolers, 86, 95, 96
Prescription. *See* Medicine
Presentation, 179–180, 187–189
Preteens, 86, 95–96, 106–107
Private home, 141–142, 190–191
Public transportation, 116–117, 131
Punctuality, 175, 191

Race. *See* Persons of color
Real-estate broker, 122, 124
Reasoning style
  cultural differences, 74–78
  styles, 75–77
Religion, 23, 41–44
Repatriation
  children, 106–107
  contact with host country, 107–108
  personal, 105–106
  professional, 104–105
Residence permit, 119–120
Restaurants, 154, 160, 189–193.
    See also Banquet

Safety, 158–159
Sales (shopping), 136
Salespeople, 136
Same-sex couples. *See* Sexual orientation
School, 132–133
School records, 217
Scientists, 37
Servants. *See* Domestic employees
Sex in Chinese culture, 142
Sexual orientation, 102, 153–154
Shopping, 134–136
  bargaining, 134–135
  clothing, 135–136
  credit cards, 134, 138
  drugstore, 135
  grocery store, 134
  hours, 135
  open-air markets, 134
  returns, 136
  sales, 136
  salespeople, 136
  supermarket, 134, 135

Single persons, 99
Smoking, 158
Social relations
  cultural differences, 53–54, 70–74, 139–141, 147–149
  dating, 142
  etiquette, 146–147
  gifts, 141
  guest in private home, 141–142
  sexual orientation, 153–154
Speech. *See* Presentation
Sports, 152–153
Spouse
  moving abroad, 82, 87–89
  stay-at-home parent, 88
  working while abroad, 88–89
Status, 67, 69–70
Subway. *See* Public transportation
Supermarket, 134, 135

Taiwan, 39–40
Taoism, 37, 41, 42
Taxi, 131
Teenagers, 86–87, 95–96, 97, 106–107
Telephone
  for business communication, 167, 175–176
  cards, 128
  cellular, 127–128
  equipment, 126, 129
  from hotel, 128, 129
  installation, 123–124, 127
  international calls, 127, 128
  Internet access, 107, 126, 176
  local, 128
  long distance, 128
  pager, 127–128
  placing calls, 128
  in post office, 128, 129
"Third-culture kids." *See* "Global nomads"
Tibet, 43
Time, 166, 184–185
  cultural differences, 55–57
  punctuality, 175, 191
Tipping, 160
  restaurant, 160
  taxi, 115

Toast (drinking), 192–193
Toddlers, 85
Toilets, 118
Train. *See* Public transportation
Translator. *See* Interpreter
Transportation. *See* Bicycle;
    Car; Driving;
    Public Transportation;
    Taxi
Travel advisories, 217
Traveler's checks, 137

Utilities, 123–124, 126

Vaccination. *See* Immunization
Video equipment, 108
Visa, 112, 215, 218
Voice mail, 175

Water, 126, 156, 157, 158
Weddings, 143–146
Weights and measures, 118
Will, 217
Women
    in business, 167–169
    cultural adaptation, 100
Work unit, 165–166